HEDGE FUND INVESTMENT MANAGEMENT

This book is dedicated to my adorable son, Michael Sheldon Nelken,
who is on his way.

HEDGE FUND INVESTMENT MANAGEMENT

Edited by

Izzy Nelken

President,
Super Computer Consulting, Inc.

ELSEVIER

AMSTERDAM • BOSTON • HEIDELBERG • LONDON • NEW YORK • OXFORD
PARIS • SAN DIEGO • SAN FRANCISCO • SINGAPORE • SYDNEY • TOKYO
Butterworth-Heinemann is an imprint of Elsevier

Butterworth-Heinemann is an imprint of Elsevier
Linacre House, Jordan Hill, Oxford OX2 8DP
30 Corporate Drive, Suite 400, Burlington, MA 01803

First published 2006

British Library Cataloguing in Publication Data
A catalogue record for this book is available from the British Library

Library of Congress Cataloguing in Publication Data
A catalogue record for this book is available from the Library of Congress

ISBN-13: 978-0-7506-6007-5
ISBN-10: 0-7506-6007-4

For information on all Butterworth-Heinemann publications
visit our web site at http://books.elsevier.com

Printed and bound by MPG Books Ltd., Bodmin, Cornwall

05 06 07 08 09 10   10 9 8 7 6 5 4 3 2 1

Disclaimer

This book is for general information purposes only. It does not have regard for specific investment objectives, financial or tax situation and the particular needs of any specific person who might read this book. Readers should seek financial, tax and accounting advice regarding the appropriateness of investing in hedge funds whose results may be volatile with the potential for loss of all or a portion of any investment. The authors do not intend for this book to be used as the primary basis for the investment of any funds subject to ERISA or similar laws of any jurisdiction. Neither the information nor any opinion expressed constitutes an offer nor an invitation to make an offer, for an investment in, or increase, decrease or sale of, any hedge fund vehicles or the purchase or sale of any security. The authors of this book (are) (or some of the authors are) employees of hedge funds and may engage in solicitation for their investment funds.

Data contained in this book has been obtained from sources believed to be reliable, but the authors do not warrant the accuracy of the underlying data or resulting computations. Strategies discussed or recommended in this book are based on data currently available to the authors, and the authors' current evaluation. Both such data and evaluation may change over time, and the authors undertake no responsibility to update this book or otherwise to communicate with any reader regarding any part of this book that they would revise based on such new data or evaluation.

Contents

Disclaimer   *v*
Contributors   *xi*
Preface   *xvii*
Introduction   *xix*
Acknowledgements   *xxi*

1 Fixed income arbitrage   **1**
  Ellen Rachlin
    1.1   Government issued debt   1
    1.2   Asset swaps (excluding convertible bonds)   3
    1.3   Yield curve arbitrage   4
    1.4   Corporate bond arbitrage   5
    1.5   Capital structure arbitrage   8

2 Diversity in mortgage hedge fund investing   **11**
  Robert Sherak
    2.1   Introduction   11
    2.2   Some basic mortgage mechanics   12
    2.3   Varieties of mortgage loans   13
    2.4   Varieties of mortgage-backed securities   15
    2.5   Varieties of strategies   16
    2.6   Analytic methods and models   18
    2.7   Liquidity and leverage   21
    2.8   Net asset value and marking to market   22
    2.9   Hedging strategies and risk management   23
    2.10 Conclusion   24

3   Absolute returns in commodity (natural resource) futures investments   **25**
Hilary Till and Jodie Gunzberg
    3.1   Return compression in hedge funds has led to an increased
          interest in investing in commodities   26
    3.2   The Traditional case for commodity investing:
          the structural returns available in the futures markets   28
    3.3   The Updated case for commodities: the potential for
          global supply shocks and inflation   34
    3.4   Risk management in commodity investing   36
    3.5   Conclusion   40
    References   41

4   Issues in hedge funds going offshore   **43**
Claudia Woerheide
    4.1   Introduction   43
    4.2   Common considerations   43
    4.3   Setting up in the Cayman Islands   54
    4.4   List of references and readings   62

5   Structured products on hedge funds   **64**
Jaeson Dubrovay and Jean-Marie Barreau
    5.1   The Basics   64
    5.2   Evolution of structured products   64
    5.3   Types of structured products   66
    5.4   Principal protection structures   72
    5.5   Using structured products   73
    5.6   Looking ahead   77

6   Careers in hedge funds   **80**
Kathleen A. Graham
    6.1   Overview   80
    6.2   Back office careers   82
    6.3   Middle office careers   90
    6.4   Front office careers   93
    6.5   Special issues that women face   98

7   A liquidity haircut for hedge funds   **102**
Hari Krishnan and Izzy Nelken
    7.1   Introduction   102
    7.2   Valuing the hedge fund manager's contract   103

	7.3	Longstaff's method	106
	7.4	Simulating the illiquidity premium	107
	7.5	Conclusion	111
	References		111

8 **Hedge fund investing: some words of caution** **112**
Harry M. Kat

	8.1	Introduction	112
	8.2	The Available data on hedge funds are far from perfect	113
	8.3	Funds following the same type of strategy may still behave very differently	114
	8.4	Similar indices from different index providers may behave very differently	116
	8.5	The True risks of hedge funds tend to be seriously underestimated	117
	8.6	Sharpe ratios and alphas of hedge funds can be highly misleading	119
	8.7	There are no shortcuts in hedge fund selection	120
	8.8	Hedge fund diversification is not a free lunch	122
	8.9	Hedge funds do not combine very well with equity	123
	8.10	Modern portfolio theory is too simplistic to deal with hedge funds	124
	8.11	One has to invest at least 20% in hedge funds for it to make a difference	126
	8.12	Conclusion	126
	References		127

9 **On ranking schemes and portfolio selection** **128**
Massimo Di Pierro and Jack W. Mosevich

	9.1	Introduction	128
	9.2	Conventions and definitions	129
	9.3	Equivalence in a Gaussian world	130
	9.4	Ranking and risk aversion	134
	9.5	A better utility function	136
	9.6	Extension to Non-Gaussian distributions	138
	9.7	Market determination of m	140
	9.8	Modern portfolio theory	140
	9.9	Conclusions	142
	References		143

Index   *00*

Contributors

Jean-Marie Barreau has over 15 years of experience in derivatives, structured products and hedge funds investments. As Managing Director at Deutsche Bank London, responsible for global fund derivatives from 2001 until 2004. He created the Xavex Alternative Investment, a hedge fund managed account platform. From 1990 to 2001, Jean-Marie worked in the equity derivatives department of Societe Generale. He served in the SG Equity Derivatives, as head of structured products in New York from 1994 to 2001, and head of structured products in Tokyo from 1991 to 1994. He is currently creating a new alternative investment platform in London for IXIS Group.

Jaeson Dubrovay, CPA is managing director and founder of an independent investment advisory firm specializing in Fund-of-Hedge Funds (*FOHF*). In this capacity, Mr. Dubrovay advises clients on hedge fund strategies, investment process, manager due diligence, portfolio construction and building innovative *FOHF* portfolios targeted to unique market segments. Previously Mr. Dubrovay was the Chief Investment Officer of Chicago-based Carr Global Advisors, a subsidiary of Credit Agricole Indosuez, where he formed and managed four *FOHF* with diverse mandates. Prior to Carr, Mr. Dubrovay formed and managed two *FOHF* for MD Sass, a New York-based investment firm. Mr. Dubrovay began his investment career managing a diversified $1.0 billion liquid portfolio for a public European holding company, HAL Trust, which was the former owner of Holland America Line. While the company also made private equity and real estate investments, the majority of the liquid portfolio was invested in traditional stock and bond managed accounts with a 10% allocation to hedge funds. Mr. Dubrovay, who served as the chief strategist and portfolio manager, was responsible for all aspects of managing the liquid portfolio, including asset allocation, manager selection, risk management and hedging non-USD exposures. He previously held senior finance positions at HAL Trust, Squibb Corporation and Arthur Andersen & Co. He holds a BA from the University of Washington (Accounting), an MBA from Santa Clara University (Finance) with honors and is a Certified Public Accountant.

Kathleen A. Graham is a Principal with HQ Search, Inc., a retained executive search firm specializing in financial services positions – including those with hedge funds – on a global basis. She has an MBA in Finance, Analytic Finance, and Econometrics & Statistics from the University of Chicago. Her other activities include being a keynote speaker/panelist/member for the Managed Funds Association, The Investment Analysts Society of Chicago, QWAFAFEW, 100 Women in Hedge Funds, 85 Broads, and numerous other organizations.

Jodie Gunzberg has diverse experience across numerous investment strategies including equities, fixed income, real estate, and hedge funds. Currently she is employed at Ibbotson Associates Advisors as a Senior Consultant, where her main responsibilities include asset allocation and manager selection for Funds of Hedge Funds.

Prior to Ibbotson, she was employed at a long/short equity hedge fund, where she developed risk management applications and quantitative models. Before this hedge fund assignment, she engineered and co-managed a market neutral equity hedge fund at Driehaus Capital Management as well as co-managed quantitative long-only equity portfolios. Previously, she was a Fixed Income Analyst at Chicago Capital Management, where she was responsible for stress testing the portfolio and performing quantitative research for governments, agencies, mortgages and high yield bonds. Ms. Gunzberg also managed commercial real estate portfolios at Equity Office Properties and started her career as an Actuarial Associate at New York Life Insurance.

She earned her MBA from The University of Chicago with a focus on Finance, Econometrics and Statistics, and Managerial and Organizational Behavior. Ms. Gunzberg is a Chartered Financial Analyst Charterholder and holds her BS in Mathematics from Emory University. She is a member of the CFA Institute and The Investment Analyst Society of Chicago.

Harry M. Kat is Professor of Risk Management and Director of the Alternative Investment Research Centre at the Sir John Cass Business School at City University in London. Before returning to academia, Professor Kat was Head of Equity Derivatives Europe at Bank of America in London, Head of Derivatives Structuring and Marketing at First Chicago in Tokyo and Head of Derivatives Research at MeesPierson in Amsterdam. He holds MBA and PhD degrees in economics and econometrics from the Tinbergen Graduate School of Business at the University of Amsterdam and is a member of the editorial board of the *Journal of Derivatives*, the *Journal of Alternative Investments* and the *Journal of Wealth Management*. He has (co-) authored numerous articles in well-known international finance journals such as the *Journal of Financial and Quantitative Analysis*, the *Journal of Portfolio Management*, the *Journal of Derivatives*, etc. His latest book *Structured Equity Derivatives* was published in July 2001 by John Wiley & Sons.

Hari P. Krishnan is an executive director and co-director of alternative asset allocation at Morgan Stanley. He runs over $1 billion of advisory capital for high net worth individuals, family offices and institutions. He was previously an options strategist at a market making firm at the CBOE and a senior economist at the Chicago Board of Trade. Hari has a BA in math from Columbia, an MSc and PhD in applied math from Brown and did postdoctoral work at the Columbia Earth Institute.

Jack W. Mosevich joined the financial industry in 1986 at Merrill Lynch after several years as a professor of Mathematics and Computer Science. His main areas of expertise are quantitative finance, risk management, derivatives analytics and portfolio construction.

Jack's experience has been equally divided between the buy-side and sell-side. He has worked in both large corporations such as UBS, Merrill Lynch and Burns Fry, as well as smaller firms such as Stafford Capital Management and Contego Capital Management. Jack is currently a Clinical Professor of Finance in the College of Commerce at DePaul University. His recent research is concentrated on risk management and portfolio construction in both traditional and especially in the alternative asset management areas. Jack is also a consultant with MetaCryption Quantitative Finance.

In addition to his core employment Jack has been a part-time instructor at the University of Chicago Program on Financial Mathematics since its inception in 1997.

Jack possesses a Ph.D. degree in Mathematics from the University of British Columbia.

Izzy Nelken is president of Super Computer Consulting, Inc. in Northbrook, Illinois. Super Computer Consulting Inc. specializes in complex derivatives, structured products, risk management and hedge funds. Izzy holds a Ph.D. in Computer Science from Rutgers University and was on the faculty at the University of Toronto. Izzy's firm has many consulting clients including several regulatory bodies, major broker-dealers, large and medium sized banks as well as hedge funds. Izzy is a lecturer at the prestigious mathematics department at the University of Chicago. He teaches numerous courses and seminars around the world on a variety of topics. Izzy's seminars are known for being non mathematical. Instead they combine cutting edge analytics with real world applications and intuitive examples.

Massimo Di Pierro is an expert in numerical and quantitative methods applied to scientific and financial modeling. He is one of the founders and owners of MetaCryption LLC.

Dr. Di Pierro is currently full-time Assistant Professor at the School of Computer Science, Telecommunications and Information Systems of DePaul University in

Chicago. He teaches graduate students regularly, and topics include Monte Carlo Simulations, Parallel Algorithms, Network Programming, and Computer Security. Dr. Di Pierro is one of the leading developers of the Master of Science in Computation Finance at DePaul.

He has published more than 20 papers in different fields and a number of software products including MCQF (a software library for financial analysis) www.fermiqcd.net (a toolkit for parallel large scale grid-like computations), Spider (a web content manager used by the United Nations).

Dr. Di Pierro earned a Ph.D in Physics from the University of Southampton in UK and has worked for three years as Associate Researcher at Fermilab.

Ms. Rachlin is a Managing Director, and is a member of the Asset Allocation and Risk Management team and the Investment Committee at Mariner Investment Group, Inc. Ms. Rachlin was formerly a Director and founding member of Deerfield International Administrative Services, Ltd. Her responsibilities included overseeing sales, marketing and product development. Prior to Deerfield, Ms. Rachlin was Co-Head of the IBJI Agent Department at both New Japan Securities International and Aubrey G. Lanston & Co., Inc. overseeing sales and trading of international fixed income products into the Americas. Prior thereto, she was a Managing Director and a Director at S.G. Warburg and Co., Inc. and S.G. Warburg, plc. in the fixed income department. Ms. Rachlin also traded fixed-income arbitrage for 5 years at Citibank, N.A. and Government Arbitrage Co. She has written several chapters for financial textbooks edited by Frank J. Fabozzi on economics and investment management, as well as other articles for finance journals. She holds an AB economics degree cum laude from Cornell University, an MBA. specializing in finance from the University of Chicago and an MA – creative writing from Antioch University McGregor. She serves as Board Member and Treasurer of the Poetry Society of America.

Robert Sherak is the founder, portfolio manager, and CEO of The Midway Group, and a hedge fund manager founded in 2000, based in New York City. Since 1976, Bob has been involved with fixed income securities, particularly mortgage backed securities, as a portfolio manager, trader, research analyst, and a programmer. His academic training was in cognitive psychology (memory, linguistics, decision making, and artificial intelligence) and computer science.

Hilary Till co-founded Premia Capital Management, LLC (http://www.premia-cap.com) in 1998 with Joseph Eagleeye. Chicago-based Premia Capital specializes in detecting pockets of predictability in derivatives markets using statistical techniques.

She is also a principal of Premia Risk Consultancy, Inc., which advises investment firms on derivatives strategies and risk management policy.

In addition, Ms. Till is a strategic advisor for Prism Analytics, a developer of advanced statistical methods useful in the analysis of hedge fund performance.

Ms. Till is an Advisory Board member of the Tellus Natural Resources Fund and serves on the Curriculum and Examination Committee of the Chartered Alternative Investment Analyst Association. She also serves on the Steering Committee of the Chicago chapter of the Professional Risk Managers' International Association.

Before co-founding Premia Capital, Ms. Till was Chief of Derivatives Strategies at Boston-based Putnam Investments. Her group was responsible for the management of all derivatives investments in domestic and international fixed income, tax-exempt fixed income, foreign exchange, and global asset allocation. In 1997 for example, the total notional value of derivatives structured and executed by her group amounted to $93.2 billion.

Prior to Putnam Investments, Ms. Till was a quantitative analyst at Harvard Management Company (HMC) in Boston. HMC is the investment management company for Harvard University's endowment.

She has BA in Statistics with General Honors from the University of Chicago and a MSc in Statistics from the London School of Economics (LSE). She studied at LSE under a private fellowship administered by the Fulbright Commission.

Ms. Till's articles on commodities, risk management, and hedge funds have been published in the *Journal of Alternative Investments, AIMA (Alternative Investment Management Association) Journal, Derivatives Quarterly, Quantitative Finance, Risk Magazine, the Singapore Economic Review,* and the *Journal of Wealth Management.*

She has also contributed chapters to the following edited books: *The New Generation of Risk Management in Hedge Funds and Private Equity Investments* (co-author, Euromoney, 2003), *Intelligent Hedge Fund Investing* (Risk Books, 2004), *Commodity Trading Advisors: Risk, Performance Analysis, and Selection* (co-author, Wiley, 2004), *Core-Satellite Portfolio Management* (McGraw-Hill, 2005), *Hedge Funds: Insights into Performance Measurement, Risk Analysis, and Portfolio Allocation* (co-author, forthcoming Wiley, 2005), and *The Handbook of Inflation Hedging Investments* (co-author, forthcoming McGraw-Hill, 2005).

Claudia Woerheide is Chief Executive Officer, Transcontinental Fund Administration, Ltd. (TFA). With 10 years of experience in alternative investments as a fund administrator, investment manager, fund consultant and being on the board of directors of other hedge funds, Ms. Woerheide has contacts with an extensive global network, insights into different styles of funds, and first-hand knowledge of valuation and accounting issues related to hedge funds. Ms. Woerheide has been the pioneer of TFA since its founding in 2001, responsible for building its infrastructure, including financial operations and business processes.

Ms. Woerheide holds masters degrees from the University of Vienna and the University of Illinois in Urbana-Champaign. She was a visiting scholar at the

University of Chicago for a year and also attended classes at the Illinois Institute of Technology's Center for Law and Financial Markets.

During her earlier years in the financial industry, Ms. Woerheide wrote a weekly column on foreign currency for *Das Wirtschaftsblatt*, Austria's premier business journal.

Ms. Woerheide has also been an invited speaker at various conferences, most recently at the 2004 Asian Finance Society conference in New York.

Preface

Several years ago, we used to speak of Hedge Funds as some mysterious instruments that were quite esoteric. Nowadays, approximately 10,000 hedge funds have about $1 trillion under management and they have become an "industry". We have to consider the effects of that industry on the financial markets at large.

We are beginning to get a better understanding of the forces that drive the returns behind these funds. This book illustrates these trends.

Introduction

The hedge fund industry has certainly grown in the past several years. Recent estimates report about 10,000 hedge funds with approximately $1 trillion under management. In the recent past, investors have relied on hedge funds to produce nice positive returns with low standard deviations. However, as I write this, in May 2005, year-to-date returns are negative in many types of hedge funds. No doubt, this will impact the industry.

In this book, we have assembled a collection of top experts to discuss various topics related to hedge funds.

Ellen Rachlin has contributed a chapter about fixed income arbitrage, while Robert Sherak has written about mortgage hedge funds. Hillary Till and Jodie Gunzberg have written about commodity (natural resources) hedge funds. Going offshore is the topic of Claudia Woerheide's chapter, while structured products related to hedge funds are discussed by Jaeson Dubrovay and Jean-Marie Barreau. Careers in hedge funds is the topic of Kathy Graham's chapter, which includes a special section on women's issues. Hari Krishnan and Izzy Nelken (myself) discuss the liquidity premium in hedge funds. Harry Kat tells us that choosing a winning hedge fund is much tougher than it looks. Finally, Jack Mosevich and Massimo Pierro discuss ranking schemes as applied to hedge funds.

Acknowledgements

Many thanks are due to the authors who have participated in the book. They have contributed time and effort. In addition, Mike Cash, the publisher was very instrumental in getting the book to print. Finally, my family was kind enough to allow me the time to put this book together.

Chapter 1

Fixed income arbitrage[1]

ELLEN RACHLIN

1.1 GOVERNMENT ISSUED DEBT

1.1.1 Basis trading (cash versus futures)

The basis arbitrageur seeks to opportunistically buy or sell sovereign bond futures against purchasing or selling short a weighted basket of cash bonds. The cash bonds will be deliverable by virtue of the contract specifications as set by the futures exchanges (i.e. Chicago Board of Trade (CBOT), London International Financial Futures Exchange (LIFFE)). The arbitrageur will typically purchase futures and sell the cash bonds at spreads that are expected to profitably converge at delivery. Rarely does the basis trader wait until delivery to take a profit. Generally, they play the divergences or dislocations that occur during the quarterly delivery cycles.

Usually, until delivery, one would expect the relationship between the cheapest to deliver bond and the futures contract to track breakeven levels. Therefore, if the futures contract and the cheapest to deliver bond deviate, the dislocations would tend to be temporary. But as the yield curve changes the bond which is cheapest to deliver may shift to a different bond issue in the delivery basket. Therefore, a basis trader has market risk, as they might not be long and short converging assets. Changes in the overall level of interest rates or changes in the shape of the yield curve may also change the cheapest to deliver bond.

Hedge funds that include government bond basis trading as part of their portfolio will typically be highly levered. The margin requirements for this trade are quite small. Therefore, it is not unusual to see gross leverage ratios of 25:1 or greater in this strategy. The primary risk of this trade is a lack of convergence between the futures and cash instruments. Even if the lack of convergence is temporary, there might be daily losses severe enough to cause the highly levered arbitrageur to

[1]I wish to thank Ed Cleaver, Murray Hood, Peter O'Rourke, Dennis Winter, Lorrie Landis and Maria Castro (Mariner Investment Group, Inc.), and Barry Campbell, and Allen Levinson (Credit Risk Advisors, L. P.) for their comments.

unwind positions to meet daily margin calls. Some causes of this situation include unusually large demand to borrow the shorted cash securities or temporarily large institutional buying interest.

Hedge fund portfolio managers may trade the basis of any maturity government note or bond for which there is an associated futures contract. There are approximately a dozen sovereign names such as the United States, United Kingdom or Japan with at least one active basis trading maturity. Some managers will look at multiple markets and maturities for attractive trading opportunities. Others will focus on one market and only one or two maturities.

The cheapest to deliver bond is the one with the highest implied repo rate. The implied repo rate is the rate of return that can be earned if one were to purchase a deliverable cash bond and finance it to delivery against selling a weighted amount of futures contracts. The implied repo rate is based upon the prospective income which could be achieved based on the current term repo rates, the bond prices and the coupons of the bonds if one positions long the cash bond and finances it to delivery of the futures contract against shorting a weighted amount of futures contracts.

As interest rates change, the value of cash bonds net of financing to the delivery of the futures contract will change as well. Yield curve shifts will change the relative value of the cash bonds in the delivery basket to one another. This will change the net financing cost to delivery term of the futures contract as well.

What this means is one cannot count on a given cash bond being cheapest to deliver for the delivery term of the futures contract. Therefore, the arbitrageur usually hedges for interest rate changes with other bonds in the basket by taking positions in those bonds. For example, the basis trader may have shorts in the first three cheapest to deliver bonds against a long in the futures contract. Because these positions are bets or synthetic options on which bond will be the cheapest to deliver, the trader may purchase out of the money puts and calls. These puts and calls will be exchange traded and will hedge the positions against changes in the yield curve. The probability that the curve will shift or that interest rates will change to a given level can be quantified in terms of optionality or into a dispersion of prices that are likely to occur in the delivery window. The trader will assess these probabilities and create hedges accordingly.

The basis arbitrageur must consider all the dynamic changes that can occur up until the delivery dates. They must also quantify the current repo rates, trading levels, option values, and so forth before ascertaining if there is a profitable cash/futures convergence opportunity.

1.1.2 Issue trading

Issue trading or issue arbitrage is similar to basis trading as the goal is to seek convergence opportunities between similar issues on the curve that have deviated in price beyond their financing and yield curve adjusted fair values. Unlike basis trading where cash and futures must converge to a fungible status with the cheapest to deliver bond, issues along the government bond yield curve are not fungible.

Issue trading focuses on cash bond instruments within generally a 6-month average maturity differential. The trader will seek out securities that deviate from a smooth yield curve return either by virtue of being rich or cheap. The trader quantifies this by extrapolating from all the issues on the relevant yield curve what the value of each time period is worth.

The trader will then ascertain a period of time for which this trade should adjust to its fair value. The adjusting factor usually is that capital is attracted to cheap not rich securities as it attempts to enhance its total return. One last piece of analysis remains which is to value the financing or carry charges associated with buying the cheap security versus selling the dear one. Frequently, the security shorted is the nearby on the run or active benchmark security (e.g. the 10-year note, 2-year note, etc.). While shorting the active issue can be treacherous, time generally works in the traders favor as the current issue ages towards off-the-run status. This financing cost is usually a negative carry cost. The trader then must adjust the spread by converting this cost into basis points.

The trader will examine the remaining spread after adjusting for the curve and for carry to ascertain if the security suspected to be relatively cheap is in fact so. If this is the case, the trade will be entered and locked up on financing for a term, say 1–3 months.

Issue trading may be conducted in one or many currency markets for which there is a well-developed repo market and adequate liquidity. The issuance must be sizable and regular to create a liquid secondary trading market. The idea behind issue trading is to avoid yield curve exposure as much as possible. For example, an issue arbitrageur would be unlikely to buy an off the run 5 year against shorting the current 2 year.

1.2   ASSET SWAPS (EXCLUDING CONVERTIBLE BONDS)

Asset swaps isolate interest rate and maturity or duration of a given asset from its credit exposure. Any fixed rate asset can be swapped. Leverage is deployed to create a short term (under 3 month) bet that the credit spread over London interbank lending rate (Libor) will change during this time period.

Typical strategies involve government bonds or agency credits, but a wide variety of corporate credits can be used as well if attractive financing rates are available.

The asset swap arbitrageur will typically seek to obtain a spread that is advantageous to what can be achieved in the cash markets or that is priced cheaply to an implied future curve. Generally, one obtains this advantage in the financing or repo markets through term specials. Term specials are usually quoted as a borrowing rate for 1 week–3 months. These specials allow the arbitrageur to gain a term rate (up to 3 months or even longer) that is lower than general collateral for this time period.

(The repo market provides financing for the leveraged trader who is deemed creditworthy by lenders who are generally banks and investment banks. The trader that seeks financing or leverage will post the financial assets that they wish to borrow or lend as collateral. The lender will charge an interest rate for the agreed upon term. At the end of that term, the collateral position is returned to the trader.)

In a typical transaction, the arbitrageur selects to purchase a security that is cheap relative to other securities of similar credit and duration as well as to Libor. The arbitrageur monitors repo rates concurrently for the best term rate. The forward price of that spread is then ascertained for its relative cheapness at the end date of the term repo agreement.

For example, consider an FNMA 5-year security. Assume that the arbitrageur has affirmed the cheapness of this security relative to other FNMA securities. The arbitrageur will purchase the FNMA 5-year security and lend it in the repo market for some term rate. In addition, the arbitrageur will purchase an interest rate swap with 5 years duration. These transactions constitute the asset swap "package". The arbitrageur has isolated the credit exposure of FNMA alone for the duration of the term repo.

Let us review how this is achieved. A 5-year FNMA security is purchased, which entitles the holder to receive semi-annual coupon payments from FNMA for a 5-year term at which time FNMA will repay the principal of the note. A 5-year interest rate swap is purchased, which entitles the holder to receive a semi-annual floating rate payment based on 6-month Libor in exchange for semi-annual fixed rate payments. The repo allows the holder to borrow money, which covers the cost of purchasing the security, as long as the security purchased is posted for collateral.

The coupon payments are hedged, as is the duration of the FNMA. However, the credit spread of the FNMA over the Libor curve remains unhedged. This exposure remains until the maturity of the repo. At that time, the trade is unwound as the contract to borrow money expires. This is not to say that the trade cannot be terminated early or replaced. Usually the arbitrageur will look for the next asset swap opportunity.

As mentioned earlier the asset swap strategy is most often deployed in the liquid government bond markets. In doing so, the aim is to create a spread trade between the government bond curve and the Libor curve.

1.3   YIELD CURVE ARBITRAGE

This strategy is more like an outright trade than an arbitrage per se. The trader that deploys this strategy does not bet on convergence or divergence but on the shape of a sovereign yield curve. This strategy is more macroeconomic in nature and would likely center on expectations for a change in central bank monetary policy.

Consider an example of yield curve arbitrage within the US Treasury market. If the yield curve trader detects that an interest rate change is likely, they will either buy or sell a short maturity U.S. Treasury security and take the opposite position in a maturity or risk weighted amount of a longer maturity US Treasury security. If the arbitrageur senses that the near term course of rates as imposed by the Federal Reserve (through a change in the discount rate) will be lower and that the current yield curve is not priced to lower rates, the arbitrageur will "buy the yield curve". That is to say they will purchase a shorter maturity sovereign debt instrument and simultaneously sell a longer-dated instrument of the same credit. If they suspect that the Federal Reserve will increase rates and that the current yield curve is not priced to higher rates, the arbitrageur will "sell the curve", which is to say that they will sell a short maturity instrument versus buying a longer dated one.

Most likely, the more imminent or apparent a rate change is, the more likely the rate change is built into the current shape of the yield curve or discounted by the market. The yield curve trader usually looks ahead to the medium term, 3–6 months (not weeks) when deciding if the yield curve reflects future rate changes. The yield curve trader will position trades in the forward interest rate derivative market. The forward yield curve as priced in the derivative markets (e.g. eurodollars or swaptions) often provides richer opportunities for prospective central bank rate changes not discounted by the market. Yield curve traders will often position a complex structure of multiple yield curve bets within one sovereign yield curve.

Another strategy that the yield curve trader might deploy is called a butterfly. The trader may feel that part of the yield curve is mispriced to both its shorter and the longer maturities. In this case, the trader would either go long the front spread and simultaneously short the back spread or vice versa. The weighting or amounts bought and sold would be in amounts that leave the trader with little to no market exposure. However, these strategies can and often do mimic outright market moves in the short run.

The difficulty in yield curve arbitrage strategies is twofold. Not only must the trader predict the future course of rates but also they must ascertain if that course is already priced into current interest rates. The trader must consider the forward rate curve as predicted by current rates and they may consider historical yield curve shapes at various historical short term lending rates such as the discount rate.

1.4 CORPORATE BOND ARBITRAGE

Corporate yield spread arbitrage is a new and growing strategy with many sub-strategies. The opportunities in this strategy have increased as the issuance in the global corporate bond markets have increased. A corporate bond can be viewed as an interest-bearing instrument with a default option attached. The bondholder has purchased an interest-bearing instrument which pays a fixed rate of return and matures at par unless the company which issues the instrument incurs financial distress. The bondholder is also short a put option on the assets of the company where the bondholder receives a spread (or option premium) in exchange for the company being able to put the assets of the company to the bondholders in the event of default. This put option will expire worthless if the company meets its bond maturity obligations. However, if the issuing company reaches a near default situation or when the franchise value of the company falls below the total of value of the company's outstanding debt, then the bondholders may exercise this option via a restructuring transaction and claim a share of the company's equity ownership.

A corporate yield spread arbitrageur will value corporate bonds in a way that expresses this view. They will consider corporate bonds as a credit free debt instrument plus a default option which is priced at an appropriate spread over the risk free rate. Not only cash instruments will be considered for long and short positions but derivatives as well. These may be single credit reference entities or sub-indicies which are groups of credits. The single reference entities or credit default swaps allow the arbitrageur to purchase or sell the same credit considered in the cash markets but at perhaps a cheaper or richer price. (Below is a discussion of corporate bond basis trading, which describes the decision process by which an arbitrageur would prefer a cash or derivative instrument on the same credit.) The sub-indicies, which contain multiple names, are a subset of one of the broader indicies such as the CDX investment grade index. The sub-indicies allow for the broader hedging of a trading book.

Information on the risk free rate component is readily available. Pricing on the default option is part quantitative and part qualitative. In short, it is more art than science. The current market price of that option is ascertainable from the price of the corporate bond, but the fundamental or the equilibrium value depends on the degree of default risk of the issuing company and must be estimated or assessed. It is therefore, subjective.

The objective in valuing the differences between the current price and the value of the default options for various bonds is to build an arbitrage portfolio or "book". The arbitrageur will purchase those bonds whose default options are cheap to their value and sell those that are rich.

Returns on bonds exhibit skewed distributions – limited upside and larger downside risk. In addition, corporate bond markets are subject to shocks and as a result, diversification is the hallmark of all good corporate yield spread arbitrageurs. Another feature of this strategy is that the ratings of the longs and shorts in the arbitrageur's book will be similar so as to avoid unnecessary credit risk. Lastly, credit risk can vary dramatically from issuer to issuer. The arbitrageur needs to assess the riskiness of long and short positions (the betas of each position) to ensure that the net position of the book is reasonably hedged. That is to say that a portfolio that has similar notional amounts of long and short positions can be net long or short depending on the riskiness of individual positions. An additional complication is that "credit betas" are not stable over time, nor do they behave consistently in tightening versus widening market conditions.

Other techniques deployed in this strategy include index arbitrage, corporate bond basis trading, and correlation trading. Index arbitrage involves the trading of a corporate bond index versus a diversified basket of single name bonds reflective of the credits in the index traded. Typically, the arbitrageur will short a tradeable index or short a cash bond index through a total return swap. (A bank dealer will exchange payments based on the performance of the index with the trader being short. They charge a libor-based fee.) The longs are selected using a variety of means. These may include methods as described above as used by the yield spread arbitrageur or a more macro process whereby the arbitrageur favors a concentrated industry selection. The arbitrageur can be viewed as attempting to beat a corporate bond index.

Corporate bond basis trading is similar in spirit to the government bond basis trading discussed earlier in this chapter. In this case, the corporate bond basis trader will go long or short a corporate bond and hedge it with a credit default swap. A credit default swap is a contract whereby the holder or purchaser has the right to deliver one of the debt obligations as defined in the deliverable basket upon the event of default. Because the price of a credit default swap trades in tandem with the credit spread over government bonds of the same currency, it can be arbitraged against the cash corporate bond of the same credit. Typically, the bond will be swapped into a floating rate credit to remove the systematic interest rate risk to more easily match the properties of the credit default swap. At times due to supply and demand imbalances in the cash markets, the relationships between corporate cash bonds and credit default swaps of the same credit become dislocated. The arbitrageur will assess the likely timing of the convergence and cost of carry to maintain the position during the expected time to convergence. (The arbitrageur may, of course, position for a divergence of this relationship, although that is less typical.)

Index correlation trading or correlation trading is a quantitative strategy. The main indicies for credit such as the Dow Jones CDX.NA.IG, an investment grade index, or the Dow Jones CDX.NA.HY, a high-yield corporate bond index, are treated as structured products and tranched into first loss to senior tranches. These tranches are assigned percentages. These percentages dictate the default percentage of the index the holder is exposed to in the basket of names that comprise the index. The holder of the first loss piece will absorb the loss of capital commensurate with the first names to default in the basket up to a dictated percentage of the corporate names in the basket. The holder of the next tranche experiences a capital loss due to defaults in the broader reference index.

Proprietary groups have developed models to determine the amount of risk that the assets in the index transfer to the various structured tranches. The level of risk can vary based on a change in default probability of the constituent firms, a change in spread for the firms or a change in the correlation of default risk for pairs of firms in the index. These relationships can be quite complex to measure effectively and can have important relative value considerations for different tranches. For example, an increase in default correlation will have a negative effect on the value of higher tranches and positive effects on the value of lower tranches. There are several approaches for using tranches in investment strategies:

1. Traders position trades based on perceived deviations between actual trading levels and risk levels dictated by their models (relative value trades).
2. Outright positions can be taken within the index based on projected changes in correlation rates, spreads or default risk – which will influence different tranches differently.
3. Tranches can be used as an effective (cost, liquidity) way to hedge other credit positions (cash or derivative). In doing so the deltas (sensitivity of tranche price to a change in the underlying index) of the tranches must be estimated effectively.

In summary, corporate bond arbitrage offers many different types of arbitrage opportunities. Some of these sub-strategies will ultimately be a more dominant part of corporate bond arbitrage trading than others mentioned here in the future.

1.5   CAPITAL STRUCTURE ARBITRAGE

Capital structure arbitrage is a stressed/distressed security trading strategy that considers the entire capital structure of the company. It is not entirely a fixed income arbitrage strategy. Equities, equity derivatives and convertible securities are considered when deploying this strategy. The capital structure arbitrage trader seeks mispricings within a company's capital structure. These may occur between senior and subordinated traunches of debt or between the equity and certain debt issues. The trader anticipates that a catalyst or event will correct the perceived mispricings.

The arbitrageur will isolate companies that have a varied capital structure and are experiencing or expected to experience difficulties. These companies are often rated below investment grade. Companies that have experienced a destabilizing shock such as fraud are often candidates for a short bias strategy, while companies expecting an industry or specific recovery are candidates for a long bias strategy.

The arbitrageur will likely have a trade book which includes capital structure arbitrage positions on several companies. But let's examine how such arbitrages are constructed. The arbitrageur will identify a company that is expected to undergo financial change. They will examine various scenarios that are likely to develop over the near term, within 3–6 months or sometimes even sooner. The arbitrageur will determine an expected value for the securities in the capital structure of the company under each scenario. (The arbitrageur will have to develop an expected price on each security under each scenario.) Generally, the arbitrageur ascribes rough probabilities to each outcome which are priced with their "scenario prices" to determine if there exists a profitable arbitrage opportunity.

The arbitrageur identifies the securities or groups of securities they wish to position long and short. Generally, they will order the securities by payout priority in the event of default or "seniority" from most senior to most junior. They do so by carefully researching each issuer's bond indentures, loan and inter-creditor agreements. The arbitrageur must have an understanding of bankruptcy recovery priorities to be consistently successful.

The most senior obligations are debt instruments guaranteed by the full credit of the company and/or secured by a lien on some or all of the issuer's assets, followed by senior subordinated debt. In a highly complex corporate structure, examining operating company versus holding company and/or subsidiary levels of debt and equity is often an important consideration. Parent companies or subsidiary guarantees as well with specific collateral pledges are also key determinants of ultimate realizable value at each level of the capital structure. (Obligations at foreign subsidiaries may or may not be affected by Chapter 11 filings.) The equity of the company or equity-like securities are last in payment priority. In addition to this consideration, the arbitrageur will consider nearest term maturities, which are referred to as "maturity-priority debt" or contractual priorities, to further identify the repayment priority (senior or junior) of potential bond claims. Because the corporate debt considered in this strategy is issued against the value or credit of a company experiencing financial distress, the arbitrageur will have to not only consider what a given security will yield but if it will yield anything at all.

The typical arbitrage involves the long positioning of senior securities in the capital structure of a company against being short more junior securities. This is a bearish scenario position. (However, the positions can be reversed for a bullish or improving credit trade.)

It may be useful to create an example trade situation and only consider its debt instruments for simplicity's sake. An ideal situation for a capital structure arbitrageur is to identify a company that is stressed due to some difficulty or disruption experiencing cash flow problems, and their debt (junior through senior) is trading at similar levels on a yield curve-adjusted basis. (Assume the liquidity of each debt issue is fairly similar.) In this ideal situation, the trader would buy its senior debt and sell its junior debt. Should the adverse financial event occur or be expected to occur, the senior bonds, which the arbitrageur is long may decline in price as much as 20 – 30 points, while the junior bonds or short position may decline as much as 50 – 60 points. The arbitrageur will profit as long as the relative weights or amount of debt purchased versus sold allow for the capture of the point decline differential of the end prices.

This strategy deploys very little leverage and often none at all due to the rather large potential price changes. In this regard, this strategy differs from the other strategies considered as *fixed income arbitrage*.

Chapter 2

Diversity in mortgage hedge fund investing

2.1 INTRODUCTION

The US mortgage market represents over eight trillion dollars of outstanding loans, making it one of the larger classes of debt.[1] Most of this debt has been securitized and is actively traded in *over-the-counter* markets as it is not listed on any exchange. The major investors and traders in mortgage-related securities include bank portfolios, savings and loan institutions, mortgage bankers, the portfolios of Fannie Mae and Freddie Mac, insurance companies, index-fund managers, and institutional bond dealers along with their proprietary trading operations.[2] Only a small percentage of hedge funds are involved in mortgage-related securities. Hedge fund managers hold and trade just a fraction of this market.

Any mortgage loans are *pooled* or *packaged* and may serve as the collateral for Collateralized Mortgage Obligations (CMOs), which are *structured* into several, sometimes over 100, bonds (tranches), each with its own priority to receive principal, interest, or prepayments from the underlying loans. This effort technological feat is a marvel of contemporary financial engineering.

An interesting feature of US mortgages is the borrower's right to prepay the loan. A borrower prepays when he moves (e.g. purchases a larger home) or *refinances* (e.g. replaces an existing loan with another that allows him to borrow more money,[3] to borrow at a lower rate, or to borrow with lower monthly payments). The mortgage loan investor is *short* the borrower's option to prepay. The CMO, as a whole, is short this same option, but its individual tranches may be differentially harmed (or even benefit) by the untimely exercise of this option. Many mortgage-related securities effectively amplify these effects. Additionally, a few of the lower rated (non-AAA) tranches may be differentially effected by the actual default and

---

[1]See www.bondmarkets.com for more details.
[2]Demand for mortgage product by Real-Estate Investment Trusts (REITs) and Collateralized Debt Obligations (CDOs) has grown in the past few years.
[3]This is called a *cash-out* refinancing.

recovery rates of the underlying mortgages. Derivatives based on mortgage-related securities may amplify or mute prepayment and credit risk.

The diversity of mortgage loans, structures (tranches), and investment strategies, has allowed for a broad assortment of mortgage hedge funds.[4] In addition, as opportunities come and go in the market, the portfolio composition of a given fund may change over time. Some managers use short-term trading strategies designed to take advantage of price dislocations, while others may employ long-term buy-and-hold strategies by finding cheap securities and realizing high yields on those securities over time. Some may be more dependent on current income (carry). In addition, managers may attempt to hedge with respect to changes in interest rates, volatility, and prepayments. This chapter outlines some of the elemental components of mortgage hedge fund management and places them in a hierarchy of loan types, bond structures, and strategies. In this effort, we emphasize risk and imply rewards with the overall goal of encouraging an appreciation for the diversity of mortgage-related hedge funds.

2.2   SOME BASIC MORTGAGE MECHANICS

A typical fixed-rate mortgage binds the borrower to a monthly fixed (level-debt) payment. The payment includes interest and a fraction of the loan principal, which increases over the payment period as the loan amortizes. There may be additional initial and ongoing payments for the appraisal, mortgage insurance, title insurance, and local taxes. A servicing fee is embedded within the interest payment for the entity responsible for bill collection, the *servicer*. This servicer forwards principal and interest payments from the borrower to a trustee responsible for calculating and distributing payments to investors. When mortgages are delivered into pools guaranteed by the Fannie Mae,[5] Freddie Mac, or Ginnie Mae, a monthly *guarantee fee* is also embedded in the borrower's interest payment.

If mortgage borrowers never defaulted, curtailed,[6] or prepaid, then little would distinguish a mortgage security from an AAA amortizing bond. However, mortgage borrowers have the option to prepay their loan at any time. While there is some predictability in how borrowers will prepay in the future, there is a good deal

---

[4]The investment category, of "mortgage backed security hedge fund," we suggest, is best used to categorize a manager skill set or investment opportunity set. Performance, opportunities, and particularly risk evaluations for two different funds are rarely similar.
[5]Fannie Mae, Freddie Mac, and Ginnie Mae are collectively referred to as the Agencies. Fannie Mae, Freddie Mac, and the Federal Home Loan Bank (FHLB) are collectively referred to as Government Sponsored Enterprises or (GSEs). Ginnie Mae is not a sponsored enterprise; it is supervised by a part of the US government, the Department of Housing and Urban Development (HUD).
[6]A partial prepayment is called a curtailment. Curtailments will not typically change future payments or rate of payments for the mortgage, but instead reduce the term (maturity) of the loan.

of forecast risk as well. The largest driver of prepayments is the current level of mortgage interest rates. A borrower who pays 6.35% on a 30-year fixed-rate mortgage will be able to reduce his monthly mortgage payment if mortgage rates fall by a significant amount, e.g. to 5.75%, as he will likely close out his existing mortgage and replace it with one at the lower rate. As long as the current mortgage rate is low enough to cover the fixed costs and transactions costs of refinancing, borrowers can benefit by refinancing. In a refinance transaction, a borrower prepays all remaining principal on the current mortgage and takes out a new mortgage at the prevailing mortgage rate. While no principal is lost when a borrower refinances, the investor cannot control the timing of principal repayment. As the example illustrates, prepayments are highest when both interest rates and returns on reinvesting the principal are lower.

If a mortgage loan is foreclosed, the mortgage servicer can arrange for the underlying property to be seized and liquidated. For the end investor, this event can be as innocuous as a prepayment for Agency pools[7] and for the higher rated tranches of Non-Agency CMO. For a smaller focused portion of the mortgage market, the lower rated and unrated tranches of Non-Agency CMOs, this can be detrimental if the full value of the mortgage is not recovered.

2.3   VARIETIES OF MORTGAGE LOANS

This section describes the reaches of the mortgage market and presents an informal classification scheme. The scheme employed here is oriented toward the everyday language usage of the mortgage professional, simplified for this brief discussion.

In addition to the amount of the loan and borrower's interest rate, mortgages vary for the following characteristics:

- *Asset type*. Mortgages for one to four family unit homes, co-op apartments, and condominiums are called *residential* loans. Mortgages for apartment complexes along with office buildings and shopping malls are called *commercial* loans and are often sold in deals called Commercial Mortgage Backed Securities (CMBS). While CMBS deals have many characteristics in common with residential MBS, the sector is different enough to demand specialized expertise for proper valuation. Another large sector of the market is generically known as Asset-Backed Securities (ABS). ABS covers a potpourri of products backed by a wide range of collateral. The two areas with the most in common with residential MBS are home equity loans (second mortgages) and subprime primary residential loans mentioned above. Credit risk plays an important role in valuing these mortgages.

---

[7]The Agencies guarantee the timely payment of scheduled and unscheduled (prepaid) principal and interest to the pool investors.

Other bonds in the ABS universe may be backed by credit card receivables, auto leases, mobile homes, aircraft, boats, property leases, and franchise loans. Many mortgage hedge funds include CMBS and ABS securities in their portfolios.

- *Credit quality.* The largest share of the mortgage market is comprised of residential loans of '*A*' quality credit. These *prime* quality mortgages are further subdivided into A and Alternative A (Alt-A). Defaults rates are expected to be less than 2% per year, even in a stressed economy and housing market. Most mortgages are considered to be of A quality. Alt-A is a vaguely defined category that has A-quality attributes, but may describe loans bordering on subprime quality. Below prime credit is the world of subprime mortgages. There is no official rating system for grading subprime mortgages, and rating agencies have differing guidelines for credit classification. Subprime mortgages are graded B, C, or D. Default rates in lower-quality subprime mortgages can exceed 20% per year. Securitizations backed by subprime mortgages are usually called as ABS and are not covered in this chapter.

- *Conforming and non-conforming.* The Agencies guarantee pools of loans smaller than a certain size (conforming limit), set annually by the Federal Government's Office of Federal Housing Enterprise Oversight (OFHEO). The current conforming limit in 2005 is $359,650 for single-family homes (50% larger in Alaska and Hawaii). Loans below this limit that fit within the other Agency guidelines are called *conforming* loans, otherwise they are called *non-conforming* mortgages. Non-conforming mortgages above the conforming limit are called *jumbo* mortgages.

- *Amortization term.* Most mortgages amortize over a 15- or 30-year schedule. Mortgages with other terms of amortization (e.g. 10, 20, 25, and 40 years) are less common.

- *Interest payment type.* Mortgages may have a fixed rate coupon, adjustable rate coupon (e.g. 1.5% over 1 month LIBOR), or a combination of both. A combination is known as a hybrid and offers the borrower a mortgage with a fixed-rate coupon for some term, typically 3 or 5 years, after which the mortgage becomes adjustable for the subsequent 27 or 25 years. A popular innovation in the mortgage market is interest-only loans. A typical interest-only mortgage may have an underlying interest rate that is fixed, adjustable or hybrid and amortize over 30 years. The key difference is that for a fixed period, e.g. 10 years, the borrower, at his discretion, may pay interest (and no principal) as part of the monthly mortgage payment. After 10 years, the monthly payment increases to include loan principal amortized over the remaining 20 years of the loan term. Hence, for the first 10 years of the mortgage, the borrower gains no equity in the home (except through possible appreciation in the property value).

- *Other loan attributes.* Various attributes of loans have been shown to be good indicators of future prepayments or defaults including loan age (the number of months since the loan was originated), loan-to-value (LTV) ratios, and borrower credit scores that are used to differentiate mortgages into more refined product types. These include, but are not limited to, property type (Single Family, Condo, or Multi-Family), occupancy (Owner-Occupied, Second-Home, or Investor), as well as geography. In particular, location of the residence also matters at the state and even county level as some regions have mortgage or property purchase taxes which may vary, and regions may experience varying degrees of home price appreciation. Such attributes contribute to different prepayment, and recovery behavior.

2.4 VARIETIES OF MORTGAGE-BACKED SECURITIES

Raw, *un-securitized*, loans are regularly sold into bank portfolios. Of the remaining loans, conforming mortgages are securitized as Agency securities while non-conforming mortgages (Jumbo or Alt-A) are securitized as Non-Agency securities. Conforming mortgages are usually bundled into pools (sizes can vary from under 1 million to over 25 billion dollars) into a larger *specified pool* market. Each pool trades according to the characteristics of the underlying collateral, with pay-ups relative to the TBA[8] futures market for pools that exhibit desirable prepayment profiles. In addition, mortgage servicing rights, a fee paid by borrowers to the servicing (bill collection) entity are regularly securitized and sold to investors can be traded.

The TBA market is the largest and most liquid sector of the mortgage market. Liquidity is concentrated around the current coupon mortgage. For instance, if the current mortgage rate for the current month is in the 6% neighborhood, mortgage originators would be creating the bulk of their pools with a 5.5% coupon (the difference between the 6% mortgage coupon and the 5.5% pool coupon covers servicing and Agency guarantee fees). Because of its liquidity, hedge funds and other mortgage players have found TBAs to be an effective hedging instrument for less liquid mortgage securities as well as a worthwhile primary investment.

Of higher complexity are the mortgaged structured products called CMOs.[9] CMOs are defined by *rules* that parcel mortgage cashflows into various types of tranches. Pools of conforming loans as well as non-conforming loan packages are regularly

---

[8]This is an abbreviation for 'To Be Announced'. This important futures market for conforming mortgages, technically a forward market, plays a central role in the mortgage industry. It is the main trading reverence point for many mortgage-related securities. Because of the time needed to settle a loan, mortgage originators can sell forward newly originated mortgages. The exact pools are not known until a date several months in the future when the seller of the TBA must inform the buyer the pools being delivered. What is known beforehand with some accuracy is the amount, pool coupon, and original maturity of the loans the originator will close and be able to deliver to the buyer. Delivered pools must conform to relevant Agency guidelines, and good delivery specifications are laid down by the Bond Market Association.

[9]Many of which are Real Estate Mortgage Investment Conduits (REMICs).

aggregated into CMOs (see footnote 9). The simplest type of structured cashflow is known as a strip. A strip is a bond that comes in two complementary types: interest only (IO) and principal only (PO). The IO holder receives interest income from the underlying pools, and the PO owner receives only principal from the underlying mortgages. Arbitrage-free pricing principles suggest that the prices of the principal and interest sum to the value of the pools underlying the strips. The risks of the two derivatives are quite different. For illustrative[10] purposes, if we assume underlying loans were priced at $100 while the PO and IO were priced at $80 and $20, respectively, and all the underlying mortgages prepaid, the PO holder would receive $100, the remaining principal balance, while the IO holder would receive nothing.

CMOs, another type of structured mortgage product, are defined by *rules* that parcel mortgage cashflows into various types of tranches. Banks and other investors typically purchase derivatives with cashflows that are more regular, predictable, and lower yielding. The remaining derivatives, which absorb most of the prepayment risk, are regularly purchased by mortgage hedge funds. These bonds, sometimes called mortgage derivatives, are very sensitive to prepayments as prevailing mortgage rates change.

To satisfy investor demand, some CMO structures will create floating-rate bonds from fixed-rate or hybrid mortgages. As a by-product of this activity, the CMO structures will also create complementary bonds with a coupon that moves in the opposite (inverse) direction from the floating-rate bonds. These derivatives are called inverse floaters (which pay the bond hold some principal from the underlying loans) or inverse interest-only bonds (which pay only interest from the underlying loans).

In the Non-Agency world, packages of loans are often structured so that the largest part of the cashflows carries an AAA credit rating. Credit subordination absorbs defaults up to a substantial, 'safe' level in order to receive an AAA rating from one or more of the bond rating agencies. The AAA bonds may have three or more levels of credit subordination (with the lowest level being unrated). Cashflows from the AAA part might then be structured along the lines of an Agency CMO in some of the ways previously discussed.

2.5   VARIETIES OF STRATEGIES

Hedge funds[11] aim at superior risk-adjusted returns by employing trading and investing strategies more sophisticated than those used by the typical investor. These strategies can require large fixed costs and depend on extensive market expertise,

---

[10]This is a very unlikely event as most pools have over a 100 loans. Prepayment of 20 loans per 100 in a given month, even in times of very competitive mortgage rates would be highly unusual.
[11]The proprietary trading desks of several institutional security dealers operate are often involved in the same trades and strategies as mortgage hedge funds.

advanced analytical software, and models. In addition, the universe of securitized loans comprises distinct asset classes with enough diversity that unique professional expertise is needed to trade each product type. Hedge funds usually specialize in one or two classes of the mortgage loan universe, but sometimes invest in more than one sector for three reasons: (1) overlap of the trading and valuation/risk framework is common across different products and does not require the entire fixed cost of the valuation/risk framework to be duplicated with the additional of new products to the portfolio; (2) portfolio diversification – different products exhibit different risk profiles; (3) expertise in several sectors allows an investor to choose among products as they become rich or cheap, depending on the theme of the week in the capital markets. In addition, a portfolio manager may employ treasury securities, interest rate swaps, mortgage swaps, interest rate caps and floors, and options on the aforementioned instruments as hedging instruments or primary investments.

In this section, for discussion purposes, we group hedge fund strategies into categories.[12] Many funds can employ a variety of strategies; others specialize in a particular strategy investing in a narrower set of securities backed by a narrower set of mortgage loans.

- *Directional/macro strategies* use mortgage-backed securities to 'bet' on the overall direction of rates. For example, most Interest Only securities go up in price as long term interest rates go higher.[13] Macro traders will use these types of securities as alternatives to interest rate futures and options when the look relatively cheaper.
- *Technical strategies* often rely on getting in front of supply and demand imbalances. For example a trader may perceive that investment inflow into mortgage funds from Asian investors, bank portfolios, or indexed managers is temporarily higher than the availability of specific categories of certain mortgage products. In other instances the hedge fund manager may recognize, or accentuate a supply shortage in a specific mortgage forward contract (e.g. Fannie Mae 6.5% deliverable next month). Here the hedge fund investor purchases the product in demand and sells a similar, perhaps cheaper, product, so that the trade is less sensitive to interest rate movement. These positions may be substantially levered and have investment horizon that range from one day to several months.
- *Relative value strategies* may estimate the fundamental richness or cheapness of similar securities or look at the historical pricing of similar securities. For example, TBA contracts deliverable into the 30-Year Freddie Mac 5% securities

---

[12]These are categories are not mutually exclusive. Additionally there are many varied substrategies within each of these categories.

[13]IO prices should improve as the expected refinancing in a higher rate environment will diminish. IO prices also can be differentially sensitive to volatility term structure. Lower volatility generally leads to higher prices.

may be either fundamentally or historically cheap as compared with the one deliverable into a 15-Year Fannie Mae 5.5% contract. The hedge fund investor will look to buy the cheap TBA and sell the richer contract. Another set of trades, commonly called basis trades involve simultaneously buying or selling combinations of TBAs, interest rate Swaps, US Treasuries, and Agency debt.[14] These trades tend to be levered and have a short-term horizon.

- *Absolute value (prepayment) strategies* typically involves the purchase of a cheap security and the capture of that cheapness over time through a variety of hedging techniques. Often the cheapness is due to the mis-pricing of the mortgagor's prepayment option that is amplified by the particular structure of a CMO tranche. The origins of this mis-pricing are manifold; these markets tend to be illiquid, and modeling expertise and analysis vary among the different kinds of mortgage securities investors. Furthermore, cashflows are structured into a CMO, the demand for one kind or security, allows a complementary structure to be created cheaply. These investments tend to have multi-year horizons, low to moderate leverage, and low liquidity. Hedges for these investments, however, tend to be liquid and levered.

- *Absolute value (credit) strategies* typically involve the purchase of lower and unrated tranches of Non-Agency CMOs. These strategies also have multi-year horizons, low to moderate leverage and low liquidity. An evolving credit default swap market can be used to hedge these investments. Credit default swaps backed by particular tranches may also be *arbitraged*. Many of these securities are not only sensitive to the underlying loans, default recovery rates, and regional economic conditions, but benefit from higher than expected levels of prepayments.

The four categories of non-directional strategies are often called *market-neutral*, a vaguely defined category, particularly for hedge funds. Market-neutral strategies attempt to hedge a portfolio's overall directional exposure to interest rates. Their risks and returns are generally unrelated to the equity, currency or commodity markets.

2.6 ANALYTIC METHODS AND MODELS

Several methods are commonly used to evaluate the risks and rewards of a mortgage-backed security. Understanding the assumptions and weaknesses of different valuation techniques is perhaps *the* most important skill. After all, the determination of risk measures (such as TBA hedge ratios) is based upon the *valuations* of

---

[14]These trades tend to be done in a 'duration neutral' fashion, that is, effort is made to keep the trades relatively insensitive to interest rates and volatilities. The process of maintain this neutrality (delta hedging) is exacerbated by the fact that mortgage sensitivities change as other rates change. Additionally, the sensitive as estimated by models may differ than the actual market moves.

complementary investments in one or more combinations of regimes of rates, pre-payments, and default/recovery environments.

The profile of future prepayments of mortgage-backed securities depends on the path of future interest rates. The two basic tools are static analysis and option-adjusted spread analysis. In essence, both tools provide techniques to generate paths of future interest rates. Given an interest-rate path, a prepayment model is used to forecast monthly cashflows of principal and interest. For credit-sensitive securities, a default/recovery model may also be employed to forecast severity of losses.

- *Static analysis*. In static analysis, an analyst specifies one or more possible paths for future interest rates, including discount rates and mortgage rates, and examines prepayment behavior and possibly default behavior of the loans underlying the security being analyzed. Common assumptions include (i) the constant scenario, in which interest rates are assumed to remain constant for the life of the bond; (ii) the forward scenario, which stipulates that interest rates evolve according to the prevailing forward curve; and (iii) up and down scenarios, which is a shift up or down of, say, 100 basis points of the constant or forward curves. Analysts have been known to be more creative, particularly when studying certain structured derivatives, and examine scenarios capturing rotations and twists in the forward curve, whipsaw patterns, which have interest rates fall and then rise over some short period, and many others. Static analysis' strength is that it allows an analyst to study several interest rate paths in detail.
- *Option-adjusted spread analysis*. One limitation of static analysis is that the paths are predetermined. A more sophisticated analysis is called option-adjusted spread[15] (OAS) analysis, an implementation of Monte Carlo simulation. This mathematical (stochastic) model describes the evolution of interest rates and is used to generate a number of simulated interest rate paths that are perturbations around the forward curve. Along a single path, the prepayment and default models generate monthly cashflows for the underlying collateral. The same experiment is repeated for, e.g. 500 sample interest rate paths. Each path represents a possible future interest rate path. Given the price of the security, the option-adjusted spread is a single number that rationalizes the known price of the security with its average value calculated by the model, where the average is taken over the set of simulated interest rate paths.[16] OAS is a single number that describes,

---

[15]This in effect considers the *option* of the borrower to prepay in many interest rate environments and *adjusts* yield *spreads* accordingly.

[16]More precisely, given a mathematical description of a security and assumptions governing prepayments and credit defaults, the interest rate model is used to define the expected value of a security in the probabilistic sense. Monte Carlo analysis as described here is a shortcut method used to evaluate the complicated integral that defines the expected value.

under some assumptions, the richness or cheapness of a given security. Essentially, a positive OAS implies that once hedged against the forward LIBOR rates, a security will have positive returns, while a negative OAS means the opposite. This methodology is also commonly used to calculate measures of interest rate sensitive, such as option-adjusted duration. However, standard OAS analysis does not account for all risks of buying and owning a given security, such as liquidity risk (described below) and model risk (bias in the interest rate, prepayment, or default models). Interpretation of this analysis requires skilled analysts who can evaluate the various shortcomings of the methodology and their impact on securities based on different collateral and different structures. What interest rate simulators have in common is a method to project 'reasonable' future monthly interest. These projections are derived from current and forward Libor (and sometimes US Treasury or Agency rates and derivative instruments) as well as interest rate volatility inputs taken from market-traded options such as swaptions and interest rate caps and floors. Interest rate models differ in their method to project rates. They also vary in how they deal with unusually low and high interest rates.[17]

- *Prepayment models*. A key input into both static and OAS analysis is the prepayment model. Prepayment models attempt to capture a borrower's propensity to prepay their mortgage principal arising from several sources. First, when prevailing market mortgage rates are lower than the borrower's current mortgage coupon rate the borrower may refinance the remaining mortgage principal. Second, general housing mobility when borrowers change residences, generally for job-related or family-related reasons, is said to cause turnover. Third, a borrower may wish to shorten his mortgage term by partially prepaying mortgage principal. This type of transaction is known as a cash-out refinance. Prepayment behavior, which depends on economic conditions prevailing mortgage rates, can be estimated from historical data that includes information on the characteristics of the borrower, the home purchased, and the type of mortgage taken out as well as descriptions of mortgage rates and other economic variables at the time of origination. In general, prepayment data are deficient in important areas. For instance, they do not include information about the borrower such as age, tenure in the home, number of children, and up-to-date financial status. Second, they reflect responses to past mortgage and economic conditions. Out-of-sample conditions such as the 40-year lows in mortgage rates recorded in mid-2003 can only be inferred using limited historical data. Third, historical data cannot cap-

---

[17]Interest rate simulators continue to evolve, and models in common use just a few years ago are now considered substandard. A wide variety of interest rate models are available to investors, some of which are developed in-house, while others are supplied by commercial vendors or institutions such as Citigroup, J.P. Morgan, Bear Stearns, or Lehman Brothers.

ture the evolving nature of the retail mortgage lending. New kinds of mortgages offer new temptations to borrowers, and technological improvements in processing mortgages continues to lower the cost of mortgage origination for mortgage bankers and innovations such as the internet are making it cheaper for borrowers to locate lower-cost mortgages than those typically offered by the neighborhood mortgage retailer. Although prepayment models are commonly calibrated to historical data using statistical techniques, prepayment analysts typically tune models to their views of how existing mortgages will respond to new mortgage products and how the changing cost of origination will influence future prepayments. The ability to adjust models to evolving views of the market is an important mortgage hedge fund management skill.

• *Default and recovery models*. To analyze mortgage credit risk, a wide variety of models have been created. Such models are at the core of the mortgage business for the bond rating agencies who do not directly address the issues of mortgage refinancing but grade bonds based upon scenario analysis for each loan involved in a securitization. Like prepayment models, credit models are based upon historical data that capture defaults and recovery rates in various levels of detail. Mortgage hedge fund investors typically pay close attention to details such as the age of the mortgage, borrower credit score, debt to income, and loan to value ratios, the quality of the mortgage originator and servicer, and the kind of property being mortgaged. Economic scenarios, particular to the location of the property, are developed, and default and recovery rates are estimated. These estimates feed into a security cash flow model that incorporates rules for how funds are passed into the different tranches and present values for the security for each scenario is computed. A necessary level of analyst subjectivity weighs the importance of each scenario.

2.7 LIQUIDITY AND LEVERAGE

It is difficult and perhaps ill advised, to characterize liquidity of a security or a portfolio of securities uni-dimensionally. The most liquid sector of the mortgage-related securities is the TBA contract, mentioned above. A typical TBA has bid-ask spreads less than half of 1 tick (1/32 of 1%) or 0.015625% in sizes of over billion dollars. Margin requirements on these contracts are often less than 2%. Individual mortgage derivative securities such as interest-only tranches, who sizes are typically less than 10 million dollars, can have bid-offer spreads of over 5% (320 times that of a TBA contract) and margin requirements of 20% (10 times that of a TBA). In periods of mortgage market stress, such as 1998, bid-asked spreads for TBAs reached 0.25% (eight ticks) while bid-asked spreads for derivatives of 20% were reported. In such periods with extremely low liquidity, few normal trades occur, and most that are completed are in auctions of forcibly liquidated securities held by security dealers who are providing margin (financing) for funds that cannot meet margin calls. Financing for these investments is allocated by prime brokers and other security dealers with consideration of bid-asked spreads and perceived risks of each security.

Hedge funds leverage is important for two major reasons. The first is the exaggeration of profit and loss the can arise as a function of both leverage ratios and market conditions. The second is the concern that hedge fund lenders will increase margin requirements in excessively turbulent markets, just as redemptions by hedge fund investors can be expected to increase. Such conditions can produce unfortunate downwardly spiraling liquidity crunches, and were experienced by several mortgage hedge funds in 1998. These funds quickly recovered, and most hedge funds and their lenders have since become more conservative with their leverage policies.

Hedge funds' mix of investments and use of leverage vary over time. Trading-oriented hedge funds may maintain TBA positions with a nominal leverage ratio of 30:1 ($30 of security is owned for each dollar invested), and a derivative-oriented fund manager may maintain a three to one leverage of his derivative positions. The derivative-oriented portfolio, using 1/10th the leverage of the trading-oriented fund, may be riskier. Methodologies exist to equate leverage across different security and trading strategies; however, an investor in mortgage hedge funds depends on the manager for effective descriptions of the fund's financial conditions and good sense of what is a prudent level of financing.

2.8   NET ASSET VALUE AND MARKING TO MARKET

Many instruments, particularly in the value strategies, are illiquid, not exchange traded and price discovery for them is usually difficult. Pricing services generally do not have the expertise to price many of these securities (but, of course, are adequate on the liquids investments such as TBAs or Agency debt.) Some hedge funds base their net asset value calculations on their own models, 'mark to model'. Others obtain bond dealer 'appraisals' or 'marks' of a fraction of the investments periodically. Still others get more two appraisals monthly for each bond.

The adequacy of a pricing methodology is important not only in assessing a hedge fund's past returns. It should matter to a hedge fund investor in value strategies, since he is effectively purchasing the portfolio of bonds a manager has obtained at the levels (NAV) determined by the hedge funds pricing methodology. The same is a concern when the hedge fund investor exits a fund, or is diluted by subsequent investments of other in that particular hedge fund.

There is an unusual paradox for the hedge fund investor, a result of the manager's presumed or actual ability to value an investment; if these investments were readily valued the profits (arbitrage) would be diminished. However many hedge fund investors would like timely pricing transparency in a way that would <u>remove</u> the investment opportunities that could be achieved with less liquid securities.

2.9   HEDGING STRATEGIES AND RISK MANAGEMENT

Most security portfolios are sensitive to changes in interest rates, volatility, leverage, and the changes in various spreads (basis). Different approaches to hedging create another layer of variety to the basic types of strategies discussed above. Some of the major categories of risks are listed below.

- *Interest rates*. Individual investments and portfolios are sensitive to changes in LIBOR rates, mortgage rates, and other interest rates. Some securities, such as specific 6% coupon mortgage pools can move up in value about 3% for a 1% move in mortgage rates, while an interest-only security collateralized by the same pool could realistically drop 50% for a similar change in rates. Furthermore, a securities sensitivity to change in interest rates is a dynamic and sometimes subjective quotient. Curve shape is an important aspect of interest rate risk. Several kinds of securities, such as inverse floaters and inverse IOs, can be much more sensitive to short-term rates (LIBOR) than to long-term rates.
- *Spread*. There are many forms of spread risk, some of which can only be offset by changing fundamental positions or buying put and call options for extreme conditions. The most important of these is how mortgage securities perform against some set of reference securities such as swaps or treasuries. If mortgages cheapen while swaps or treasuries remain unchanged the mortgage basis is said to widen. If a swap is used to hedge a mortgage position, then a widening of the mortgage basis implies a capital loss in the position even though the position is interest-rate neutral. Interest-rate neutral means that a change in swap rates will leave the position with no change in profit as long as the spread between the swap and the mortgage position is constant. Hence, a position that is interest-rate neutral does not mean it is neutral with respect to a change in the basis spread. Many spread relationships move with factors internal to the mortgage market. For example, some drivers of spreads include changes in supply or demand of 15- versus 30-year mortgages, demand for 5% coupon 30-year TBA contracts deliverable in June versus that deliverable in July, and the relative preference for IO securities versus PO securities.
- *Volatility*. Due to the embedded option in mortgage loans, volatility is an important factor in pricing and risk management. Portfolio managers may employ options on Treasuries, Eurodollar options, swaptions, caps, and floors to manage volatility exposure.
- *Credit*. Subprime mortgage backed securities and the subordinated and equity tranches of all Non-Agency CMOs take on significant credit risk. There is not

yet a sophisticated credit default swap market as in the market for corporate and high-yield bonds. Many of these instruments are issued discounted to par (below 100 cents per dollar) and perform well when refinancing is at a sustained, high level. For other types of securities of grade A and alt-A, credit risk relative to other forms of risk is less consequential.

- *Model error*. For most strategies, a major risk is in the pricing and valuation models themselves. In the case of prepayment models, one way to measure sensitivity to model risk is by valuing investments as if refinancing, housing turnover, and so forth where 10% greater or less than expected. The level of error is, of course subjective. One way of managing this risk is to match securities which should under perform in a slow prepayment environment with securities which would outperform in the same circumstances. For example, some POs can offset IOs backed by similar loans if prepayments turn out to be faster than initial model expectations.

2.10   CONCLUSION

This chapter attempts to serve the hedge fund investors as both as an introduction to the mortgage market and mortgage hedge funds in general. A key point in this chapter is that mortgage hedge funds can be considered a single investment category in only the most limited sense. Frequently, hedge funds invest in unrelated sectors of the mortgage security universe. They specialize in different trading strategies and structures and may exhibit returns uncorrelated with one another. The level of information and analysis to become an informed mortgage hedge fund investor is not trivial, but with diligence and consideration for the diversity within mortgage hedge funds, I believe investors can find a diverse set of superior managers.

Chapter 3

Absolute returns in commodity (natural resource) futures investments

HILARY TILL[1] AND JODIE GUNZBERG

In this chapter, we introduce readers to commodity (natural resource) futures programs. We begin the chapter by describing the present investment landscape as one where return compression in a number of popular hedge fund strategies has led absolute-return investors to investigate other promising return sources. This includes the highly volatile natural-resource markets, which Lammey (2005) describes as a "paradise for speculators".

The second section of the chapter discusses how (real) *spot* commodity prices have been in a long-term secular decline, which has meant that in the past, most arguments for investing in commodities have had to rely on one of the two following rationales. An investment in a commodity *futures* program has had to (1) capture cyclical opportunities, or (2) provide an inherent risk premium that has only been available in certain futures markets. This latter concept is admittedly esoteric and will be explained later in this chapter.

In the third section we will argue that current commodity investment programs, which are designed to either capture cyclical opportunities or monetize risk premia, are still valid in the current environment. But we will further note that one can also make a plausible case for investing in commodities based on increases in *spot* commodity prices. The 1990s were marked by "a series of unusually favorable supply shocks", which may *not* be the case going forward, as O'Neill *et al.* (2004) have warned.

In the concluding section of the article, we will outline the risk management requirements for a commodity investment program, given that absolute-return

[1]Hilary Till would like to acknowledge assistance from Joseph Eagleeye, the co-founder of Premia Capital Management, LLC, in the development of some of the ideas discussed in this chapter. She would also like to express gratitude to Mr. Jerry Pascucci of Citigroup for support of Premia Capital's trading methodology.

investors require that hedge funds control downside risk rather than just "capture the premium of the asset class", as Ineichen of UBS (2003) has explained.

3.1   RETURN COMPRESSION IN HEDGE FUNDS HAS LED TO AN INCREASED INTEREST IN INVESTING IN COMMODITIES

Over the past 10 years, not only has the number of hedge funds quadrupled but also the assets under management have grown exponentially. There are currently an estimated 8,000 hedge funds, which in aggregate manage about $1 trillion. As hedge fund assets grow, one wonders whether the inefficiencies that initially brought them success will still be available to exploit. "Performance in general seems to be deteriorating. In the late 1990's, ... no one would touch a fund that did not claim to be able to make 15% a year. Now investors seem happy with a promise of high single-digit returns", noted the Economist (2004).

Exhibit 1 illustrates how in general hedge funds have underperformed the U.S. equity market and, for that matter, commodities over the 2-year timeframe, March 2003 through March 2005.

The high fees available to hedge fund managers have caused traditional managers to migrate to the hedge fund space. Unfortunately for existing hedge fund managers, those moving into hedge funds are the same investors that were on the opposite side of the trade to supply hedge funds with inefficiencies in the first place. In that case, who is going to provide the inefficiencies that hedge funds have been able to monetize? As more of the "inefficiency suppliers" move into hedge funds themselves, a natural consequence is for these inefficiencies to diminish or disappear.

As covered in Till (2004), there is nothing new about the concept of superior investment strategies proving to be fleeting. As Siegel (2003) has noted, "High-beta stocks beat low-beta stocks until William Sharpe discovered beta in 1964; small stocks beat large ones until Banz and Reinganum discovered the size effect in 1979...".

Another example has been provided by Gatev, Goetzmann and Rouwenhorst (1999). Over the period 1962–1997, they "find average annualized excess returns of up to 12 percent for a number of self-financing [equity] portfolios of top pairs". But they also find, "Pairs trading has declined in profitability dramatically from the 1970s and the 1980s to a low point at the end of our sample when the returns were sometimes negative". They hypothesize that after the strategy's discovery in the early 1980s, "competition has decreased opportunity".

Further, Agarwal, Daniel and Naik (2003) provide evidence of the capacity-constrained nature of the hedge fund industry. Using data from January 1994 through December 2000, they find, "large hedge funds with large inflows display poor

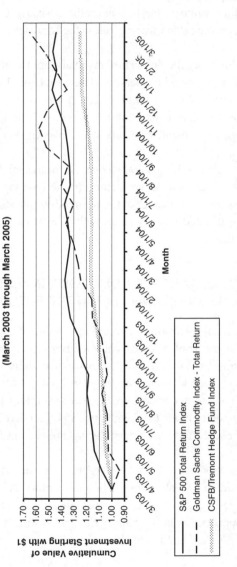

Exhibit 1 Cumulative value of an investment in US equities, commodities, and Hedge funds (March 2003 through March 2005). (Data source for S&P 500 and Goldman Sachs Commodity Index: Bloomberg; Data source for CSFB/Tremont Hedge Fund Index: http://www.hedgeindex.com; CSFB stands for Credit Suisse First Boston.)

future performance and a lower probability of exhibiting persistence. This finding is consistent with decreasing returns to scale in the hedge fund industry".

Loeys and Fransolet (2004) provide a framework for understanding which hedge fund strategies are likely to perform well in the future. Generally, the fewer hedge funds pursuing the same strategy, the less deep the derivatives market, and the more advanced the technology and trading rules, the more likely a strategy will perform well.

Of note is that at this time, the dominant financial opportunities have been in the financial rather than commodity markets. The exponential rise in financial derivatives since the late 1970s has (until recently) crowded out academic *and* practitioner interest in the commodity futures markets, leading to the present opportunities for those investment managers who have chosen to specialize in commodities.

Opportunities in the commodity (natural resources) futures markets appear to be available because of cyclical *and* secular factors. In the next two sections of this article, we will discuss the traditional case for commodity investing, which is still valid, followed by the updated case for commodity investing, which, while still unproven, is quite plausible.

3.2   THE TRADITIONAL CASE FOR COMMODITY INVESTING: THE STRUCTURAL RETURNS AVAILABLE IN THE FUTURES MARKETS

The traditional argument for investing in commodities could not rely on the historical performance of the spot price of commodities. Reinhart and Wickham (1994) write that "during 1992 the prices of commodities relative to those of manufactures reached their lowest levels in over 90 years". They further note that "the sustained decline [in commodity prices] predates our sample period of 1990–92. Using a different commodity index that begins in 1854, [another author] … documents the decline of real commodity prices during the second half of the nineteenth century".

Instead, absent predictions of inflation, the argument for investing in commodities has had to be based on one of the two following factors. A commodity manager has had to be able to exploit cyclical opportunities *or* has had to be able to take advantage of opportunities in the *futures* markets, which are different from those available in the *physical* commodity markets.

3.2.1   Structural returns due to supply usage imbalances

As discussed in Till and Eagleeye (forthcoming, 2005), if there are inadequate inventories for a commodity, only its price can respond to equilibrate supply and demand, given that in the short run, new supplies of physical commodities cannot be mined, grown, and/or drilled. When there is a supply/usage imbalance in a commodity market, its price trend may be persistent, which, in turn, systematic trend-following programs may be able to capture.

In Burghardt, Duncan and Liu (2004), researchers at Calyon Financial provided empirical evidence that trend-following systems may indeed be able to capture dynamic returns in the commodity futures markets.[2]

We will now turn to a summary of arguments concerning other structural sources of return available in the commodity futures markets, as originally developed in Till (1997).

3.2.2　Structural returns due to hedging pressure

The futures markets exist to facilitate hedging, not to forecast prices
The likely reason for the persistent returns in long-only commodity futures programs, such as those benchmarked to the Goldman Sachs Commodity Index (GSCI) or the Dow Jones AIG Commodity Index (DJ-AIGCI), has to do with the economic function performed by commodity futures markets. These markets exist to facilitate hedging, not to forecast future spot prices.

As will be further explained below, there tends to be an excess of commercial entities who are short hedgers across a number of commodity futures markets. Therefore, in order to balance the market, investors must be willing to take up the slack of the long side of these markets. And in order to be persuaded to enter these markets, investors need a return for their risk-bearing. "In effect the hedgers offer ... [investors] an insurance premium for this service", as Bodie and Rosansky (1980) put it.

In other words, investors earn an "insurance premium" for being systematically long commodity futures contracts.

In the following, we will explain the theory underlying the rationale for commodity futures' persistent returns as it was initially proposed, and then later developed, expanded and tested.

Keynes
It was John Maynard Keynes who first proposed the hypothesis that a passive investment in commodity futures should be profitable. He first published this

---

[2]Regarding their results, the Calyon researchers caution that "commodity markets tend to be less liquid than financial markets. Many [futures] managers, to get around the constraint that illiquid commodities markets would place on their trading capacity, continue to expand by decreasing the weight that commodities play in their portfolio".

theory, which became known as the "normal backwardation[3] hypothesis", in 1930 in A Treatise on Money.

One can summarize Keynes' hypothesis as follows.

Commodity prices tend to be highly volatile. This is because:

(a) demand is difficult to predict;
(b) in the short-run, the supply response for most commodities is inelastic; and
(c) Redundant inventories are prohibitively expensive to hold.

This means that if there is a miscalculation in demand, only the commodity's price can adjust in order to balance supply and demand.

With commodity prices so subject to violent fluctuations, producers will in effect pay speculators an insurance premium to lay off this unpredictable risk. Producers do so through the futures markets. Keynes (1930) explained that "[even] if supply and demand are balanced, the spot price must exceed the forward price by the amount which the producer is ready to sacrifice in order to 'hedge' himself, i.e. to avoid the risk of price fluctuations during his production period".

In other words, in order to induce speculators to assume the price risk of forward production, producers tend to sell their production forward at a discount to expected future spot returns. Commodity futures prices, therefore, tend to be downwardly biased. This is the key insight underlying both the rationale for an indexed investment in commodities as well as the main fundamental driver for a number of active commodity investment programs.

Hicks

J.R. Hicks further developed the hypothesis that commodity futures prices tend to be downwardly biased estimates of future spot prices in 1939 in his book, Value and Capital: An Inquiry into Some Fundamental Principles of Economic Theory.

A key element of Keynes' hypothesis is that it is producers who desire to use the futures markets to hedge unpredictable, volatile spot price risk. But what about consumers? Would not they be long hedgers? If one has both long hedgers and short hedgers, why should the futures price be downwardly biased?

In essence, Hicks' theory is that undiversified producers are in a more vulnerable position than consumers, who can choose among alternatives as well as time their purchases. Given that producers are more vulnerable to commodity price fluctuations, they will consequently be under more pressure to hedge than consumers. This

---

[3]In the commodity markets, when a futures contract's price trades at a discount to the spot price, this relationship is referred to as "backwardation". When a futures contract's price trades at a premium to the spot price, this relationship is referred to as "contango".

leads to a "congenital weakness" on the demand side of a number of commodity futures markets.[4]

Returns have not historically relied on a secular increase in spot commodity prices

The returns from commodity *futures* investments have often been confused with the returns from *physical* commodity investments. For example, Biggs (1994) wrote that "real commodity prices have been in a slow, gradual secular downturn, interrupted by cyclical disturbances". His article questioned the validity of commodity indexed investments.

But, as Bodie and Rosansky (1980) showed and Gorton and Rouwenhorst (2004) later confirmed, long-only commodity *futures* investments have tended to be profitable over long periods of time with equity-like returns. How can this be the case if (real) spot commodity prices have tended to decline? It is because commodity futures prices, in order to facilitate forward hedging, have historically embedded a risk premium. Over time, one monetizes this risk premium by owning commodity *futures* contracts.

Nash and Shrayer of Morgan Stanley (2004) have shown that the historical returns for a number of futures contracts have been quite different from their spot price changes. Their calculations are shown in Exhibit 2.

Nash and Shrayer's (2004) calculations appear to confirm the hypothesis that the returns from investing in commodities have *not* primarily been due to changes in spot prices, at least over the period, April 1983 to April 2004. The spot prices in Exhibit 2 all changed by at most ±3% per year. Correspondingly, the total returns from passively owning and rolling a number of futures contracts have been

---

[4]In 1939, Hicks used the intuition underlying the commodity futures contracts' "normal backwardation" hypothesis to develop his more widely known "liquidity premium" hypothesis for bonds. In this latter hypothesis, he notes that all things being equal, a lender would rather lend in short maturities since they are less volatile than longer-term-maturity bonds. On the other hand, an entrepreneur would rather borrow in a long maturity in order to fix his costs and better plan for the future. In order to induce borrowers to lend long, they must be offered a "liquidity premium" to do so. The result is that bond yield curves tend to be upwardly sloping. (Whereas, with a number of commodity futures contracts, the normal curve shape is downwardly sloping, i.e. in "backwardation".)

The common idea behind both the "normal backwardation" hypothesis and the "liquidity preference" hypothesis is that commercial entities are willing to pay risk premiums from the profits of their ongoing businesses to hedge away key volatile price risks.

This latter point was further reinforced by Holbrook Working in 1948 in his "Theory of the Inverse Carrying Charge in Futures Markets". In using futures markets, commercial hedgers have wider business considerations in mind than expressing opinions on where future spot rates will be:

> "The hedger, whose arbitrage is incidental to merchandising or processing, tends to be satisfied to take profits from his major operation and to require [futures] price relations only that they be such as not threaten him with [overall] loss".

	Annualized Return of Futures Contract (includes Interest Income)	Annualized Change in Spot Price
Crude Oil	**15.8%**	1.1%
Heating Oil	**11.1%**	1.1%
Gasoline (since 1/85)	**18.6%**	3.3%
Copper	**12.0%**	2.3%
Live Cattle	**11.0%**	0.7%
Corn	-1.9%	0.0%
Wheat	-0.4%	0.2%
Soybeans	5.7%	2.3%
Gold	-0.2%	-0.5%
Silver	-3.3%	-2.8%
Platinum	8.2%	3.1%
Soy Meal	8.8%	2.5%
Bean Oil	4.6%	2.9%
Sugar	1.8%	-0.4%
Coffee	-2.9%	-2.8%
Cocoa	-4.7%	-1.0%
Cotton	4.1%	-1.1%
Max	18.6%	3.3%
Min	-4.7%	-2.8%

Exhibit 2   Annualized return of individual commodity futures markets (April 1983 to April 2004).
Source: Based on Nash and Shrayer (2004)

10%+ per year. This latter calculation includes the interest income earned from fully collateralizing one's investment in each of the commodity futures contracts.

Whereas an investment in a commodity index has generally benefited from bearing risk that commercial hedgers desire to lay off, an active commodity program will seek to identify those times and those commodities, where one is particularly well compensated for bearing this risk.

Active commodity strategies that benefit from structural returns in the commodity markets

Exhibit 2 shows that the most fertile ground for looking for profitable opportunities has been in the energies, base metals, and livestock markets. Each of these sectors has had healthy returns over extended periods of time. (Of note is that the GSCI is majority-weighted in these three sectors.)

As explained in Till (2000), a common feature of each of these commodity futures contracts is that their underlying commodity has a difficult storage situation. For these commodities, either storage is impossible, prohibitively expensive, or producers decide it is much cheaper to leave the commodity in the ground than store above ground. As a result these commodities have relatively low inventories relative to demand.

The existence of storage can act as a dampener on price volatility since it provides an additional lever with which to balance supply and demand. If there is too much of a commodity relative to demand, it can be stored. In that case, one does not need to rely solely on the adjustment of price to encourage the placement of the commodity. If too little of a commodity is produced, one can draw on storage; price does not need to ration demand.

Now, for commodities with difficult storage situations, price has to do a lot (or all) of the work of equilibrating supply and demand, leading to very volatile spot commodity prices, which in turn leads to the classic Keynesian effects described below.

Producers and holders of commodity inventories will turn to the commodity futures markets to control or manage uncertain forward price risk. The price pressure resulting from commercial hedging activity causes a commodity's futures price to become biased downward relative to its future expected spot rate. In that situation, a long commodity futures position will have a positive expected return.

An active commodity manager will focus on those commodity markets that have produced consistently positive returns over time. Historically, those markets have included the energies, base metals, and livestock sectors. The active manager will then attempt to distill the returns in these markets even more so than an indexed program through entry and exit rules, trade construction, and downside risk management.

Since the driver of returns for the energies, metals, and livestock sectors appears to have been due to their difficult storage situations, an active manager needs to also continually monitor whether these factors are still in place. At present, this still appears to be the case. In summary, for the petroleum complex, the financing of inventories remains prohibitively expensive. For metals, the cheapest place to store them is still in the ground. And finally, livestock, by their very nature, are not storable. Once an animal becomes market weight, it needs to be brought to market immediately since further feedings are costly while simultaneously degrading the quality of the animal.

There is anecdotal evidence that pension fund investors are beginning to examine the structural sources of return in the commodity markets in order to add value to their core exposure in commodities, which in turn has been obtained by investing in commodity indices. For example, MARHedge (2005) reports that the leading Finnish pension plan, Ilmarinen Mutual Pension Insurance Company, has been examining actively managed allocations to "specialist clusters or sectors using subindices such as energies and livestock".

The final section of this chapter will address some of the unique risk management challenges that an absolute-return manager faces when designing an investment process around monetizing risk premia in the commodity markets. But before that, we will cover an updated case for commodities, which focuses on *spot* price increases as being a driver of returns in the commodity markets.

3.3   THE UPDATED CASE FOR COMMODITIES: THE POTENTIAL FOR GLOBAL SUPPLY SHOCKS AND INFLATION

Although the weakness in spot commodity prices has been "primarily of a secular, persistent [downward] nature", as noted by Reinhart and Wickham (1994), there are stirrings that we may be an entering a new era of adverse supply shocks and perhaps inflation.

For example, O'Neill *et al.* (2004) warn how the experience of the 1990s may have been unique with "crises in emerging markets and weakness in Japan and Asia ... put[ting] downward pressure on [commodity] prices and ... [increasing] the supply of savings to other markets, creating a safety valve for inflation and interest rate pressures globally". The Goldman Sachs researchers note that the "recovery in Japan and Asia has already reduced slack and begun to generate inflationary pressures".

In the following section, we will summarize the arguments for potential increases in the spot prices of the petroleum complex and base metals. Lastly, we will touch upon an inflationary analogy to the 1970s, given current monetary policy.

3.3.1   Petroleum complex: Aging energy infrastructure and Asian demand

A super spike in oil

Murti *et al.* (2005) write that investors should recognize that the "major differences between the current cycle and the [benign] 1990s cycles include the lack of spare capacity throughout the energy supply chain ... [and] the fact that Asian economies have recovered from an "once a generation" economic crisis that occurred in the late 1990s".

The Goldman analysts explain that the global "energy supply infrastructure has barely kept up with demand. Insufficient spending over the past two decades, coupled with natural growth in oil demand alongside global economic growth, has led to a steady erosion of spare capacity in crude oil production that was built up during the energy boom years of the 1970s", according to Murti *et al.* (2004).

After the energy boom of the 1970s, OPEC built their deliverable spare capacity up to almost 12 million barrels per day (mln b/d). Today it has been diminished to just about an estimated 1 mln b/d.

"Further complicating the energy supply chain is the fact that growth in global refining capacity has also been limited in the past two decades ... Refining capacity growth has been limited to Asia-Pacific and, to a lesser degree the Middle East ... with extra barrels likely to stay in Asia-Pacific due to surging demand in the region as well as product specifications that likely do not meet US and European standards", continue Murti *et al.* (2004).

No new refineries have been built in the US and Western Europe for three decades, according to Morrison (2005). Exhibit 3 illustrates the decline in spare global refining capacity.

Given the strength in demand for crude oil by the United States and China, and the lack of spare capacity in the production of crude and in refining capacity, Murti *et al.* (2005) attempt to estimate the range of crude oil prices that would suffi-ciently reduce energy consumption to balance supply and demand. The analysts note that it has to be a demand reduction that balances supply and demand since the "addition of meaningful new quantities of supply" would take 5–10 years.

The Goldman analysts predict that the range of prices required to meaningfully reduce demand is between $50 and $105 per barrel, which they refer to as a "super spike" range. The analysts look to the experience of the late 1970s and early 1980s to see what price spikes are required to create demand destruction.

The Goldman argument for the possibility of oil price spikes partly relied on continued economic growth in China and other Asian economies. This is also the underpinning for a bullish view of base metals by Citigroup analysts.

3.3.2 Base metals: A new industrial revolution in China

A super cycle in copper
The intensive industrialization in China may not only drive a super spike in oil prices but may also create a super cycle in copper prices.

The key drivers of China's metals demand are fixed capital formation, urban-ization, and domestic consumption. Writes Heap (2005), "Fixed capital formation

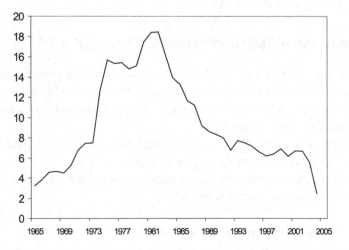

Exhibit 3 Spare global oil refining capital (mm/bpd). *Source*: Howell (2005), which was derived from an analysis by Paul Horsnell of Barclays Capital

is an important driver of metals demand in China. Fixed capital formation has increased to 40% of GDP.... Urban migration is an important driver of fixed capital formation and super cycles. In China, 10 million people per year are moving from the countryside to the cities, according to World Bank estimates, and this may increase four-fold as restrictions on the movement of labor are relaxed as required by the WTO.... At least 50%, and perhaps 75%, of China's copper demand is for domestic consumption.... China's copper demand is not export driven, nor is a result of a relocation of manufacturing capacity from other countries.... This is … an important characteristic of past super cycles".

Heap (2005) defines a super cycle as "a prolonged (decades) trend rise in real commodity prices, driven by the urbanization and industrialization of a major economy".

Booming industrialization from emerging countries has historically been a super-cycle catalyst. "Super cycles [in metals] occurred in the late 1800s–early 1900s (driven by urbanization and industrialization in the USA), and in the late 1940s–early 1970s (driven by post war reconstruction in Europe and Japan, and subsequently the Japanese economic renaissance)", explains Heap (2005).

Heap illustrates two past super cycles in Exhibit 4.

3.3.3   Excessive monetary stimulus: The 1970s revisited

Finally, in addition to the issues discussed above, Howell (2005) points out how excessive monetary stimulus has contributed to the high returns of commodities in the past. "Negative real interest rates in the 1970's contributed to a commodity boom". Real short-term interest rates are now negative in the USA again and in China, which is illustrated in Exhibit 5.

3.4   RISK MANAGEMENT IN COMMODITY INVESTING

If an absolute-return investor finds that the arguments for a potential increase in spot commodity prices are plausible, then that investor should consider either a commodity-index investment or an actively managed long-only commodity vehicle as part of their overall portfolio.

For further value-added, the investor should also consider including strategies that take advantage of both cyclical opportunities and the risk premia that are embedded in certain commodity futures markets. These latter strategies do not rely on a secular boom in commodity prices.

3.4.1   The need for downside risk protection

If a hedge fund investor elects to invest in an index product, then that investor realizes that he or she will earn the inherent return of the asset class, will be able to do

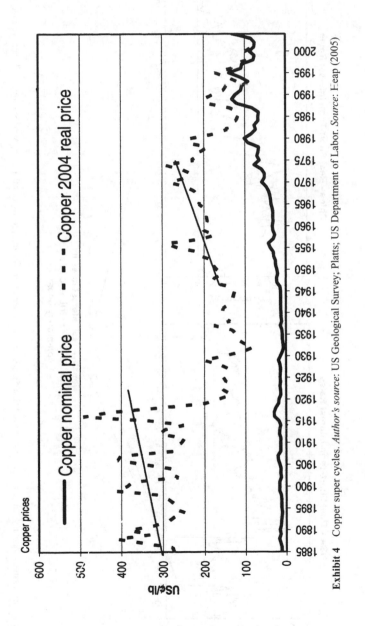

Exhibit 4 Copper super cycles. *Author's source:* US Geological Survey; Platts; US Department of Labor. *Source:* Heap (2005)

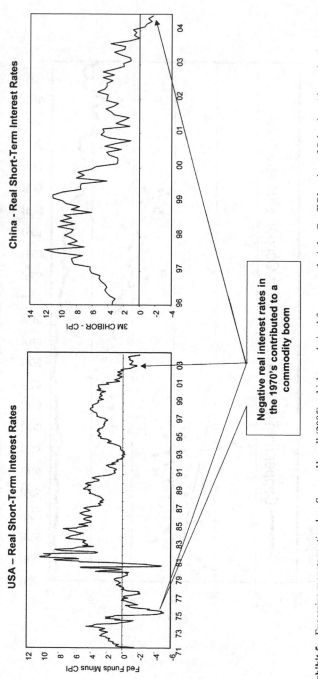

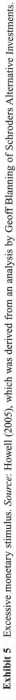

Exhibit 5 Excessive monetary stimulus. *Source:* Howell (2005), which was derived from an analysis by Geoff Blanning of Schroders Alternative Investments.

so cheaply, but will not be provided with any downside risk protection. It will be the responsibility of the investor to time their investments in commodity indices so as to avoid downside risk.

Instead, if the investor chooses an actively managed commodity program, then that investor expects the potential downside of this investment to be carefully managed. For example, Ineichen (2003) notes that long-short equity sector hedge funds have opportunity sets that are correlated to their respective sectors, resulting in the active sector funds having returns that are correlated to their sector indices. But even so, these hedge funds control their downside risk so that ultimately their returns compound at a higher rate than their respective sector indices. The same expectations hold for active commodity programs in controlling downside risk.

In a designing a risk management program for a commodity investment, one needs to address both idiosyncratic risks and macro risks. Idiosyncratic risks include those unique to a specific commodity market. Examples include simulating the impact of the discovery of Mad Cow disease in the US on live cattle futures positions as well as examining the impact of the New York harbor freezing over on the price of near-month heating oil futures positions. Macro risks include discovering those risks in the portfolio that can create inadvertent correlations amongst seemingly uncorrelated positions. Examples include simulating the impact of a September 9, 2001 event on a portfolio that is long economically sensitive commodities as well as examining the impact of surprisingly cold weather at the end of the winter on a portfolio of energy positions.

3.4.2 Payoff profiles and sizing

Historically, hedge fund investors have expected a long-option-like payoff profile from their futures investments. If instead these investors wanted consistent returns with the rare chance of very large losses, they can already do so by investing in arbitrage strategies.

Some opportunities in the commodity futures markets have short-option-like payoff profiles. One example is weather-fear premia strategies. In these trades, which can be found in the grain, tropical, and natural gas futures markets, a future price is systematically priced too high relative to where it eventually matures. This occurs before a time of unpredictable weather such as the Brazilian winter or summer-time in the US Midwest and Northeast. In the case of the Brazilian winter, an extreme frost can damage Brazil's coffee trees. In the case of the US summer-time, an exceptional heat-wave can impair corn pollination prospects as well as stress the delivery of adequate natural gas supplies for peak air-conditioning demand.

Over long periods of time, it has been profitable to be short these commodity markets during the time of maximum weather uncertainty. But during rare instances, these strategies can have very large losses, which create classic short-option-like profiles.

If one includes short-option-like strategies in an absolute-return futures program, then the sizing of these trades needs to be reduced compared to the sizing of trades with long-option-like profiles in order to preserve the program's overall long optionality.

In a previous section, we discussed commodity markets that were difficult-to-store. These markets have a tendency to experience periodic mini-price spikes since their inventories tend to be relatively low compared to demand. If there is any miscalculation in demand or supply, one cannot draw from negative storage so the only lever that can balance supply and demand is price, which can move violently upward. As a result, long positions in difficult-to-store commodities tend to have long-option-like payoff profiles. These are markets whose sizing need to be sufficiently large to provide the overall portfolio with its long optionality.

3.5 CONCLUSION

As there has been in the past, there are opportunities to earn an insurance premium for being long of certain commodity futures contracts (which the Goldman Sachs Commodity Index is majority-weighted in), which do not rely on a secular increase in spot commodity prices.

That said, the current environment is one of risks of adverse supply shocks because of aging US and European energy infrastructure as well as expanding Chinese demand. This may boost the potential returns of investing in a commodity futures program due to increases in spot commodity prices.

Hedge fund investors expect the downside of each of their actively managed investments to be carefully managed. As a result, an active commodity manager needs to be alert to potential scenarios that could create inadvertent correlations within his or her portfolio, which could thereby unexpectedly increase risk.

Historically, hedge fund investors have also expected their futures investments to provide a great deal of long optionality. One way of achieving this is to choose to invest in those sectors that have typically had difficult storage situations, including the energies, base metals, and the livestock sectors.

As opportunities have eroded in a number of hedge fund strategies, absolute return investors have started to consider investing in (natural resource) commodity futures programs. One may expect this interest to intensify if we are indeed in "a major bull market sustainable for many years", as predicted by Fusaro (2005).

REFERENCES

Agarwal, V., Daniel, N. and Naik, N. (2003) Flows, performance, and managerial incentives in the hedge fund industry, Working Paper, Georgia State University and London Business School, July 24.

Biggs, B. (1994) Commodities as an investment? *Morgan Stanley/Strategy and Economics*, May 31.

Bodie, Z. and Rosansky, V. (1980) Risk and return in commodity futures, *Financial Analysts Journal*, **36**(3), 27–39.

Burghardt, G., Duncan, R. and Liu, L. (2004) What you should expect from trend following, *Calyon Financial Research Note*, July 1.

Economist (2004) From alpha to omega, *Economist.com*, July 15.

Fusaro, P. (2005) The intersection of hedge funds and the energy markets. Presentation to the Executive Risk Officers' Assembly, Professional Risk Managers' International Association, Chicago, April 27.

Gatev, E., Goetzmann, W. and Rouwenhorst, K.G. (1999) Pairs trading: Performance of a relative value arbitrage rule, Yale School of Management Working Paper, February 27.

Gorton, G. and Rouwenhorst, K.G. (2004) Facts and fantasies about commodity futures, Yale International Center for Finance Working Paper No. 04-20, June 14.

Heap, A. (2005) China – the engine of a commodities super cycle. Citigroup Global Equity Research, March 31.

Hicks, J.R. (1939) Value and Capital, Oxford University Press, London.

Howell, R. (2005) Investment Seminar, Schroders Alternative Investments Group, Commodities, Gstaad, February.

Ineichen, A. (2003) Asymmetric returns and sector specialists, *Journal of Alternative Investments*, **5**(4), 31–40.

Keynes, J. (1930) A Treatise on Money, Macmillan, London.

Lammey, A. (2005) Investors clamor for stake in bull run in stocks, commodities, *Energy Intelligence: Natural Gas Week*, April 4, pp. 1, 18–19.

Loeys, J. and Fransolet, L. (2004) Have hedge funds eroded market opportunities? JP Morgan, October 1.

MARHedge (2005) Leading Finnish pension eases into commodities, April 12.

Morrison, K. (2005) Lack of new refining capacity puts pressure on supplies of oil, *Financial Times*, March 12–13.

Murti, A.N., Ahn, L., Singer, B. and Stein, J. (2004) Super spike option value provides further upside for R&Ms, Goldman Sachs Global Investment Research, September 10.

Murti, A.N., Singer, B., Ahn, L., Stein, J., Panjabi, A. and Podolsky, Z. (2005) Super spike period may be upon us: Sector attractive, Goldman Sachs Global Investment Research, March 30.

Nash, D. and Shrayer, B. (2004) Morgan Stanley presentation, IQPC Conference on Portfolio Diversification with Commodity Assets, London, May 27.

O'Neill, J., Patel, B.C., Lawson, S., Masih, R., Wilson, D., Buchanan, M., Fuentes, M. and Purushothaman, R. (2004) Global supply shocks: is luck running out? *Goldman Sachs Global Economic Weekly*, June 23, pp. 1–12.

Reinhart, C. and Wickham, P. (1994) Commodity prices: Cyclical weakness or secular decline, *International Monetary Fund Staff Papers*, June, pp. 175–213.

Siegel, L. (2003) Benchmarks and Investment Management, Association for Investment Management and Research, Charlottesville, VA.

Till, H. (1997) The reasons to invest in commodities, Putnam Investments Working Paper.

Till, H. (2000) Systematic returns in commodity futures, *Commodities Now*, (September), **4**(3) 75–79.

Till, H. (2004) On the role of hedge funds in institutional portfolios, *Journal of Alternative Investments*, **6**(4), pp. 77–89.

Till, H. and Eagleeye, J. (Forthcoming 2005) Commodities – active strategies for enhanced return, The Handbook of Inflation Hedging Investments, Robert Greer (ed), McGraw Hill, New York.

Working, H. (1948) Theory of the inverse carrying charge in futures markets, *Journal of Farm Economics*, **xxx**(1), pp. 1–28.

Chapter 4

Issues in hedge funds going offshore

CLAUDIA WOERHEIDE

4.1 INTRODUCTION

Once upon a time in hedge fund wonderland there was a hedge fund manager who wanted to get international clients. In order to adhere to the prevailing rules of the land he knew that he had to get offering documentation and a memorandum and articles of association. Therefore, he plucked the appropriate documents from the healthiest looking tree in the land and carried them home; soon afterwards he distributed them at the right time and the right place to the right clientele; and he consistently produced the right performance numbers thereby making himself and his clients rich and content; and all of them lived happily ever after …

Wouldn't it be nice if reality could match the fairy tale? Unfortunately, all too often the setup of an offshore fund is accompanied by stories of endless delays, out-of-bound costs, angry clients, confused sponsors, conflicts of interest, and never matching time schedules of the involved parties. Evidently this is not ideal. Consequently, it will be the focus of this chapter to establish a procedure for the sponsor of an offshore fund which if adhered to should allow for the avoidance of common problems.

The secret to keeping away from cost explosion and seemingly never ending delays in time is proper preparation. It can save significant amounts of time and money if the sponsor is completely aware of the issues which need to be mastered and what type of service providers need to be selected aforehand.

This chapter will discuss general issues of consideration for the setup of an offshore fund and then outline an average application process on the Cayman Islands for the fund promoter who wants to substantially abbreviate his lead time. Nevertheless, if a sponsor starts from scratch it is realistic to assume a time investment of at least two months for drafting and finalizing the offering document and the memorandum and articles of association (the "mems & arts").

4.2 COMMON CONSIDERATIONS

Generally, hedge fund managers going offshore have already been in business onshore for some time. They might decide to become the promoter of an offshore fund either because their US fund has reached its limit, because some of his/her clients want to invest their retirement accounts, or because foreign investors have become a target group in their marketing efforts. Usually, like US citizens, foreign investors are citizens of countries with capital gains, income- and other taxes. If these investors choose to invest into a US hedge fund, they would either be double taxed or they would have to investigate whether a tax treaty between their home countries and the US exists. Understandably, there is a preference among foreign investors to select a jurisdiction without taxes as the domicile for their investment purposes. This fact puts offshore centers without taxes onto the map of the investment world and when it comes to hedge funds, the Cayman Islands in particular.

4.2.1   Taxes, laws, and reputation

It is highly recommendable to involve experienced lawyers into the setup of an offshore fund. Usually, there will be at least two lawyers involved, an onshore and an offshore lawyer. The onshore lawyer will structure the offering document and the offshore counsel will review it and prepare the memorandum and articles of association for the incorporation. If there is a large seed investor, foreign or not, he will probably also hire an attorney to represent him. In case the investor is foreign, the primary task of his lawyer will be to examine the benefits of the proposed structure in relation to the tax laws of the investor's home country and their effect on the income derived from the investment.

In cases where it turns out that the suggested structure will be adverse to maximizing income from the investment for the investor, a restructuring of the fund is recommended. For example, some countries treat income derived from dividends or income derived from interest different in their laws pertaining to capital gains taxes. Income from dividends might be taxed higher than the comparable income from interest. In this case, if the sponsor had previously planned to structure the offshore fund as a dividend paying income note, he will be well advised to reconsider restructuring his vehicle as a bond paying interest.

Because offshore funds are investment vehicles accessed by international parties, the legal system of the jurisdiction that governs the offering document and the contracts must be recognized within the international context, It is important that the laws of this jurisdiction should be easily attainable and in a language that is understood by all parties involved. The preferred hedge fund offshore domiciles at the moment are based on English Common Law or on European Civil Law.[1]

---

[1]Bermuda, the Cayman Islands, the Bahamas, and the British Virgin Islands (BVI) are based on the English Common Law; The Netherlands Antilles (Curacao) are based on European Civil Law; none of the preferred offshore hedge fund domiciles are based on the US common law style corporate laws. UK style and Civil Code jurisdictions typically request corporate records to be kept in the jurisdiction itself; (see "Offshore Jurisdictions: Choices, Challenges and Changes" in my list of refrences at the end of this article).

The investor's legal advisor will focus on whether the target domicile is recognized in his/her own country and whether there exists a large enough case law in the offshore jurisdiction's corporate and investment legal system or whether there are at least provisions that the case law of another jurisdiction may be invoked. It will be up to counsel to decide whether all contracts will be governed under the law of one jurisdiction or not.

Last but not the least, the reputation of an offshore jurisdiction matters. This is particularly true when the investor intends to resell the investment he has made into the offshore fund by repackaging it in his own home jurisdiction; thereby practically becoming the sponsor of another offering document in his home domicile and adjusting his offering memorandum so that it also fits the offering memorandum of the offshore fund. If this is the case, most often this "resale" is intended to benefit retail investors, who typically don't have detailed industry knowledge of the product they buy but they hear a lot and they read newspapers. To this extent, a jurisdiction's reputation will be of utmost importance to this investor whose success not only depends on the performance of the investment manager but also on the credibility and respectability of the jurisdiction of formation.

Taxes, the legal system, and reputation are sufficiently important topics to an investor to justify the cost of an attorney representing his interests in the structuring phase of the fund. Since the aims and ends of investors can clash when more than one large seeding investor is involved in the setup phase of the fund, it requires diplomacy to be able to ride the waves of the various competing interests without endless delays or, in a worst case scenario, the complete breakdown of negotiations. In a best case scenario, the sponsor will find individual solutions for each problem but it might not always be possible to accommodate all parties' needs and compromises will be necessary.

4.2.2   Hedge fund strategy

Another consideration is the hedge fund itself. What does it trade? Can the investment strategy also be followed in a jurisdiction that has investment restrictions? Have the jurisdiction and its service providers served similar vehicles before? Is there a corporate structure available that can house this type of fund optimally? How flexible are the available legal structures and do they protect the investor adequately? Will it be possible to administer changes once the structure has been established? How cumbersome will that be?

The above questions need to be considered by the investment manager and the sponsor together with their lawyers and offshore counsel. In general, hedge funds profit from jurisdictions that understand alternative investment, specific investment needs and have passed laws to accommodate them. In recent years, the hedge fund community has favored the Cayman Islands and Bermuda. Both are largely acquainted with hedge fund structures, special purpose vehicles, and structured notes, and the law of both domiciles makes an attempt to follow the necessities of the market.[2] However, since the Cayman setup is more cost-effective, more funds decide to register in Cayman versus Bermuda. In addition, Cayman has been as or some people might argue more creative than Bermuda. For example, beyond establishing the Cayman Stock Exchange (CSX)[3] in 1997, the latest innovation of Cayman's law makers is the "Segregated Portfolio Company".[4] It is a form of incorporation previously reserved for the insurance industry only and now extended to the fund sector and it has already attracted a lot of followers. I will discuss this type of company later on in this chapter.

4.2.3   Reputation of oversight, fund regulation and due diligence

A credible supervisory authority is relevant for a functioning financial market place. In an international context it helps parties who don't know each other to build up trust; the knowledge that an independent party is watching over the rules of the game makes it easier to invest into vehicles far away from home. Consideration will need to be given whether the proposed offshore fund can work within the regulatory frame work of the chosen jurisdiction. No supervision will deter the investor from investing[5] but too much will keep the manager from trading. Consequently, finding the right balance is essential.

Of course, regulation also costs money. Therefore, the cost of licenses for registered funds, incorporation fees and the cost of the service providers depend at least partly on the experience, size and reputation of the supervisory regulatory authority. Hence, the European offshore domiciles being the oldest ones are typically more expensive than the Caribbean islands. Within the Caribbean, prices coincide with reputation, the Cayman Islands are on top followed by Bermuda, the British Virgin Islands and the Bahamas. Curacao has not yet been chosen as a jurisdiction of choice for hedge fund managers since most of the hedge fund managers from the US feel more comfortable with the British legal system than with the Dutch

---

[2]The latest comparable statistical information available both in Bermuda and Cayman is from quarter 4, 2002. It shows that Cayman has 4,285 registered mutual funds versus Bermuda with only 1,294 such funds. (*Sources*: Bermuda Monetary Authority Quarterly Update, (2003); CIMA web site).

[3]The exchange initially provided a listing facility for offshore mutual funds and specialist debt securities. In March 1998, rules for the listing of derivative warrants had been introduced, and after that followed an expansion into depository receipts and recently into Eurobonds.

[4]See in the Companies Law (2003 Revision), section 232–248.

[5]For example if fund administration services are not licensed, then everybody with or without industry knowledge, money or morals could operate as a fund administrator and potentially harm the investors of the fund. Hence, regulation provides a safety network for the investor by keeping standards high; the US has no acting supervisory agency for hedge funds; they can administer themselves which could open them up to fraud or they can employ administrators who have no supervisory agency to report to. Accordingly, one might say that from an investor's perspective there is an additional element of comfort when an investor invests into an offshore fund.

one. In addition, the basic legal texts in Curacao are all written in Dutch. However, service providers in Curacao offer their services also to hedge funds.[6]

In practice, the question to ask from a sponsor's and investment manager's point of view is: what is too much regulation, and what is just not enough? In respect to the balance of investment restrictions versus investor protection, the Caribbean jurisdictions beat the ones close to Europe.[7]

I will discuss the categories of regulation for Cayman mutual funds as an example for the Carribean model.[8] Cayman has minimal investment restrictions and thereby offers itself as a prime place for all innovative new investment instruments.

Cayman mutual funds are governed by the Mutual Funds Laws[9] which had been originally enacted in 1993, and was last revised in 2003. The objective of the law is to protect the mutual fund investor from fraudulent service providers and to regulate each mutual fund by fitting it into four categories: licensed; administered; registered; or exempted mutual funds.[10]

In order to fall under any mutual funds category, the vehicle must issue shares which can be redeemed or repurchased at the option of the investor. Investors in these shares must be able to participate in the gains or profits of the investment, and the investor funds must be pooled with the aim of spreading investment risks among the shareholders.[11] Accordingly, closed-ended funds do not qualify and are not regulated under the law.

The Cayman Islands Monetary Authority (CIMA) oversees licensed, administered and registered mutual funds, summarized under the term "regulated" mutual funds.[12]

---

[6]The latest comparable statistics for funds registered in the Bahamas, Bermuda, BVI and the Cayman Islands is from the last quarter of 2002: Bahamas – 669 funds; Bermuda – 1,294 funds; BVI – 2,991 funds; Cayman Islands – 4,285 funds. At the end of 2004, the Cayman Islands – 4,285 funds. At the end of 2004, the Cayman Islands registered funds rose to 5,249 whereas the last available report from Bermuda (June 2003), shows a docline to 1,279 registered funds. (*Sources*: Bahamas – Securities Commission of the Bahamas, March 26, 04; Edrick Cleare [phone conversation]; Bermuda – Bermuda Monetary Authority Quarterly Update. (2003); BVI – Investment Business, Financial Services Commission. Ruth Chadwick. E-Mail message from March 26, 04; Cayman Islands – CIMA Website; the Curacao International Financial Services Association was unable to furnish statistics as to the amount of mutual funds currently registered.)
[7]This might seem like an uncorroborated statement, however supporting it would go beyond the limit of one chapter in a book. I suggest that anybody interested in learning more about the jurisdictions close to Europe starts by researching for the following investment related terminology: SICAF ("Société d'investissement à Capital Fixe", Luxembourg); UCITS and NON-UCITS regulations ("Undertakings for Collective Investment in transferable Securities", Ireland); CIF ("Collective Investment Funds", Jersey); Collective Investment Schemes, Guernsey;
[8]I do not mean to say that all other Carribean jurisdictions have the same categorization as Cayman. Each jurisdiction has its own categories which should be carefully examined before a commitment is made.
[9]The funds are also governed by the laws governing their chosen structure of entity formation, e.g. Companies Law for corporations, Partnership Law for partnerships … .
[10]Andrew Murray: "Regulation of Mutual Funds in the Cayman Islands" in: International Offshore and Financial Centres Handbook, 1999/2000.
[11]See Mutual Funds Law (2003 Revision) (2).
[12]See Mutual Funds Law (2003 Revision) (4).

Exempted funds don't need to file any documentation with the CIMA. As previously mentioned, most hedge funds would fall under the category of "registered mutual fund". This is partly already premised in the private placement memorandum of the fund since the fund's lawyer would typically advise his client to make the minimum investment no smaller than CI$40,000 which translates to US$48,780.4. Since this is a "strange" number the minimum investment is typically US$50,000. Should the fund fall below this amount, then the fund would no longer qualify for the "registered"[13] category which is the category with the least regulatory restrictions among the regulated mutual funds. The only exception to the above is that a fund could alternatively be listed on one of the stock exchanges recognized by the CIMA.[14] Otherwise, the fund might have to apply for a license[15] or become an administered fund.

---

[13]See Funds regulated under Mutual Funds Law (4)(3).
[14]Recognized stock exchanges at the time of writing this chapter (January 2004): American Stock Exchange (AMEX); Amsterdam Stock Exchange (Amsterdamse Effectenbeurs); Antwerp Stock Exchange (Effectenbeurs vennootschap van Antwerpen); Athens Stock Exchange (ASE); Australian Stock Exchange; Barcelona Stock Exchange (Bolsa de Valores de Barcelona); Basle Stock Exchange (Basler Börse); Belgium Futures & Options Exchange (BELFOX); Berlin Stock Exchange (Berliner Börse); Bergen Stock Exchange (Bergen Bors); Bermuda Stock Exchange; Bilbao Stock Exchange (Borsa de Valores de Bilbao); Bologna Stock Exchange (Borsa Valori de Bologna); Bolsa de Comercio de Buenos Aires; Bolsa de Comercio de Santiago; Bolsa de Valores de Lima; Bolsa de Valores de Caracas; Bordeaux Stock Exchange; Boston Stock Exchange; Bovespa (São Paulo Stock Exchange); Bremen Stock Exchange (Bremer Wertpapierbörse); Brussels Stock Exchange (Société de la Bourse des Valeurs Mobilières/Effecten Beursvennootschap van Brussel); Cincinnati Stock Exchange; Copenhagen Stock Exchange (Kobenhayns Fondsbors); Düsseldorf Stock Exchange (Rheinisch-Westfälische Börse zu Düsseldorf); Florence Stock Exchange (Borsa Valori die Firenze); Frankfurt Stock Exchange (Frankfurter Wertpapierbörse); Fukuoka Stock Exchange; Geneva Stock Exchange; Genoa Stock Exchange (Borsa Valori de Genova); Hamburg Stock Exchange (Hanseatische Wertpapierbörse Hamburg); Helsinki Stock Exchange (Helsingen Arvopaperipörssi Osuuskunta); Hong Kong Stock Exchange; Irish Stock Exchange; Johannesburg Stock Exchange; Korea Stock Exchange; Kuala Lumpur Stock Exchange; Lille Stock Exchange; Lisbon Stock Exchange (Borsa de Valores de Lisboa); London Stock Exchange (LSE); Luxembourg Stock Exchange (Société de la Bourse de Luxembourg SA); Lyon Stock Exchange; Madrid Stock Exchange (Bolsa de Valores de Madrid); Marseille Stock Exchange; Mexican Stock Exchange (Bolsa Mexicana de Valores); Midwest Stock Exchange; Milan Stock Exchange (Borsa Valores de Milano); Montreal Stock Exchange; Munich Stock Exchange (Bayerische Börse in München); Nagoya Stock Exchange; Nancy Stock Exchange; Nantes Stock Exchange; Naples Stock Exchange (Borsa Valori di Napoli); NASDAQ (The National Association of Securities Dealers Automated Quotations); New York Stock Exchange (NYSE); New Zealand Stock Exchange; Oporto Stock Exchange (Bolsa de Valores do Porto); Osaka Stock Exchange; Oslo Stock Exchange (Oslo Bors); Pacific Stock Exchange; Palermo Stock Exchange (Borsa Valori di Palermo); Paris Stock Exchange; Philadelphia Stock Exchange; Rio de Janeiro Stock Exchange (BVRJ); Rome Stock Exchange (Borsa Valori di Roma); Singapore Stock Exchange; Stockholm Stock Exchange (Stockholm Fondbörs); Stuttgart Stock Exchange (Baden-Württembergische Wertpapierbörse zu Stuttgart); Taiwan Stock Exchange; Tel Aviv Stock Exchange; The Stock Exchange of Thailand; Tokyo Stock Exchange; Toronto Stock Exchange; Trieste Stock Exchange (Borsa Valori die Trieste); Trondheim Stock Exchange (Trondheims Bors); Turin Stock Exchange (Borsa Valori de Torino); Valencia Stock Exchange (Borsa de Valores de Valencia); Vancouver Stock Exchange; Venice Stock Exchange (Borsa Valori de Venezia); Vienna Stock Exchange (Wiener Wertpapierbörse); Zurich Stock Exchange (Zürcher Börse).
[15]See Mutual Funds Law (2003 Revision)(4)(1)(a).

A licensed fund has the most stringent regulatory oversight. The level of scrutiny applied by the CIMA regarding the sponsors and directors of the fund is much higher than the one employed on registered funds. The prime difference between an administered and a licensed fund however seems to lie in the fact that in an administered fund the prime responsibility for the fund lies with the administrator as opposed to directly with the CIMA. Both, with registered and licensed funds, registration is processed directly through the CIMA, however, with the administered fund, it proceeds through the administrator.

The sponsor of the fund will hardly realize any difference between an administered, a registered or a licensed fund. In all the above cases he has to provide due diligence information. Only the recipient of the due diligence will change. The MF1 Form asks for specifications on all service providers, but the bulk of the due diligence inquiries is transferred to the administrator who has a statutory obligation[16] that matches the due diligence obligation of the CIMA.[17] The licensed administrator who writes the letter of consent for the fund will sign that he has performed all due diligence checks and has satisfied himself that the fund is in full compliance.[18] Hence, a registered fund will still have to undergo in depth due diligence for its directors, the sponsor, and the other service providers of the fund. In addition, the initial and future investors into the fund will have to undergo a due diligence process in line with the "Guidance Notes on the Prevention and detection of money laundering in the Cayman Islands".[19]

The Mutual Funds Law also holds a provision for "exempted funds".[20] Exempted funds are non-regulated "mutual funds". Equity interests must be held by not more than 15 shareholders in an exempted fund, and the majority of these shareholders must be able to remove the board of directors of the mutual fund. Usually, this would exclude the average mutual fund from this category because the typical mutual fund has a division into voting and non-voting shares in its capital structure. The non-voting shares are allotted to the investors and therefore the investors would not have the right to remove the board of directors of the mutual fund by vote.

CIMA will refrain from the supervision of exempted funds, however, it reserves itself the right to object to the chosen name of a fund and to request that the offering document of the fund describes all offered shares in all respects necessary for an investor to make an educated decision concerning an investment into the fund.[21]

---

[16]See Mutual Funds Law (2003 Revision) (16).
[17]See Mutual Funds Law (2003 Revision) (5) (2).
[18]While the law does not have a provision for fines or any other type of consequence for CIMA if it transgresses Section 5(2), the fine for the fund administrator who contravenes the due diligence provision is US$121,951.
[19]Guidance Notes on the Prevention and Detection of Money Laundering in the Cayman Islands, September 2003 version; Version September 26, 2003; www.cimoney.com; Anti-Money Laundering.
[20]See Mutual Funds Law (2003 Revision) (4) (4).
[21]See Mutual Funds Law (2003 Revision) (4) (1); (6) (2).

Due diligence on subscriptions into funds has become the focus of the offshore industry's ongoing efforts to enforce anti-money laundering structures onto its financial service providers. Often enough investment managers and sponsors hate this due diligence process since it involves "hassle" for the investor. They think that it is hard enough to make a sale and bothering investors with needless paperwork and painstaking identity checks cannot be beneficial to the inflows of cash into their funds. This is correct but the world after September 11th has become particularly nervous about cash flows in general and about their control in particular. If a fund is only suspected of money laundering or improper practices in any way, the financial authority of the jurisdiction – in this case, the CIMA – has the power to freeze all assets in the fund.

Obviously, nobody would ever want to experience such an incident. Transfer agents/administrators for funds have therefore developed a system that protects the fund's current investors until the incoming investors have gone through the due diligence process. The transfer agent[22] will first establish a separate bank account for all incoming fund subscriptions. This will be the "subscription account" the address and account number of which will appear in the subscription – and offering document of the fund. As long as the due diligence on a subscriber has not been completed and as long as the subscription is incomplete in relevant sections, the money must remain in this separate, non-interest bearing account. Once the due diligence process has been concluded and the subscription date is closed, the money will be transferred into the trading account of the fund.

In general, the due diligence process is time consuming. Since subscription documents are legal documents and not easily understood by everybody, many investors forget to fill out portions of the subscription form. Then the administrator must contact the subscriber and ask him/her to fill in the missing sections. The subscriber must undertake all changes on the subscription form him or herself; the administrator is not permitted to make the changes on behalf of the investor. The only blanks that are filled out by the administrator are the number of shares an investor holds in a particular series and class, whether the subscriber is eligible for "new issues", and possibly the corrected amount this investor invested; the investment amount might turn out not to be the numbers the investor gave in his application because exchange rates vary and banks take wire transfer charges; from the answers that the investor gave in the subscription application, the administrator will determine whether an investor is eligible for "new issues" or not and then allocate the appropriate share class to the subscriber.

In a scenario where the administrator does not receive all requested information from an investor, and hence is not in a position to pass a judgment on the fitness

---

[22]Typically, the administrator would be the transfer agent.

of this investor for the fund, the subscription must not be accepted. These procedures protect the other investors in the fund against contaminated money.

Investor protection is a buzz word for the offshore hedge fund community. The
average offshore setup of a hedge fund protects the end investor to a much larger
degree than the setup of a hedge fund in the United States. In most cases offshore
supervisory agencies require the involvement of independent service providers in
addition to the fund manager and the auditor. Domestic hedge funds have no
requirements to appoint an administrator,[23] who would calculate Net Asset Values
(NAVs), take in subscriptions, pay out the fees to the various service providers and
redemptions to the investors. The investment manager may do all of it himself.

International clients who frequently have never seen the investment manager
they invest their money with from face to face, most often feel suspicious of a
setup without independent service providers since it lends itself to fraud.
Some US investment managers recognize the pitfalls of this non-regulation and
voluntarily employ independent service providers to create a better control environment.

Meanwhile, the US will implement a new rule on hedge funds by February
2006. The rule will provide for some fraud control by no longer permitting hedge
fund managers might soon have to tread the path which their offshore counterparts
have already gone for the last years; namely, moderate regulation with a focus on
investor protection.[24]

---

[23]In addition, the administration business in the US can be provided by non-licensed and non-regulated
entities. Basically anybody can set up shop and sell himself as a fund administrator.

[24]A lot of hedge fund managers do what is right for their clients but some do not. Investors beware! Take
a closer look if you want to be sure: a common conflict of interest arises if a manager wants to primarily save money versus making it his/her primary objective to making the vehicle he/she manages fraud
proof. A frequently observed case is a fund with a manager who has hired his/her auditor to also provide for the monthly/quarterly NAV calculations. Of course, the fund will pay less for the annual audit
in this scenario because the auditor basically audits his/her own work. Clearly, the independence, one
of the most important qualities of an audit, is no longer given in such a case. Another scenario is the
manager who calculates his/her own NAVs, then provides them to the administrator who only distrib-
utes what the manager has forwarded to him. At the end of the year, the fund is audited by an independent auditor. This too is not the best case scenario. Apparently, in such an arrangement, the
administrator can not be held responsible for wrong NAV calculations since he/she was not in charge
to calculate them in the first place; also, it permits the investment manager to commit fraud much easier than if an independent third party were involved to compare their own monthly calculations with the
calculations of the manager at all valuation dates. Unfortunately it is more likely that the Securities and
Exchange Commission SEC – which is also the regulator for accountants/auditors – will think of a way
to regulate hedge funds in the US than that it will think to regulate the audit industry in a way to pre-
clude the above described abuses prevailing in the accounting industry in its dealing with hedge funds.
Therefore, it is currently up to the investors to protect themselves from fraud and negligence by their
managers through investigating the service provider network used by the fund and the relation of the
ownership structure of these services providers to each other.

4.2.4   Marketing and listing considerations

Before the fund chooses a custodian and instructs its lawyer to work on the offering documentation, the sponsor should consider whether the fund must obtain a listing on a stock exchange[25] or not. In order to increase its chances for getting a higher percentage of foreign investors in a certain segment of the existing foreign fund of funds population, the fund might have to undergo a listing on a stock exchange in an OECD country. In such a case, the sponsor of the fund should identify the stock exchange on which the listing will take place and then find out what requirements exist for the fund to be listed.

Stock exchanges might have requirements for investment management, minimum investment and diversification of trading instruments, leverage, custodian, auditor and more. Many choices that might seem good choices might not hold up within the logic of some exchanges. A sponsor should be particularly careful about his choice of custodian when he is dealing with the ISE. Within the US context, the ISE does not accept anything else but a custodian governed by the SEC as a custodian.[26] Sometimes, funds do not have an established custodian relationship with an entity governed by the SEC because this would not be a practical relationship given the nature of the fund; for example, this would be the case if the fund in question is a fund of funds which otherwise would only hold a bank account or if the vehicle to be listed trades futures and uses a futures commission merchant (FCM) instead of a prime brokerage. Since neither banks nor FCMs are regulated by the SEC, the ISE doesn't consider them appropriate custodians. The ISE chooses to ignore organizations like the NFA (National Futures Association) or the Federal Reserve Bank; therefore, neither banks nor FCMs are recognized as possible custodians for funds to be listed on the ISE.

The only way for a fund of funds to get listed on the ISE is by establishing a potentially unnecessary relationship with a custodian. In practice this means that the fund will open a "bank account" for which it will get a custodian contract and for which it will pay hard cash. This in turn, will result in higher fund expenses to be paid by the investors.

Typically, it is not the investment strategy which necessitates the listing but the potential growth prospects of the fund. Accordingly, the question arises for the sponsor at what time he should undergo this additional expense; if it is done right at the beginning, the private placement memorandum will not need to be changed

---

[25]In most cases the listing of the fund is done for marketing purposes. For example, Luxembourg SICAVs ("Société d'investisement à Capital Variable") are only permitted to invest a small percentage of their funds into alternative investments. However, if they are listed on a stock exchange in an OECD ("Organization for Economic Cooperation and Developement") country, this percentage becomes larger. Thus, in order to attract the investment from SICAVs some funds get listed on the Irish Stock Exchange (ISE).

[26]Of course, this is not the only requirement which a custodian must fulfill; however, it is one of the most essential ones.

later, if not, the change will constitute an added layer of expense for the fund at a later time; however, maybe the fund cannot bear any supplementary expenses at the initial stages; it all depends on the marketing prospects, the amount and type of investors and the size of the vehicle; this decision should be made by the sponsor in consultation with his/her marketing team.

4.2.5   Privacy protection

Another item of deliberation for the sponsor should be the privacy protections of the jurisdiction of choice; this is important because the end investors in the fund might expect their privacy to be protected from the public; in particular, this means whether a company's ownership can be searched for by the public or not.

Many hedge fund managers choose the Cayman Islands for their privacy laws. Privacy in the Cayman Islands is protected under the "Confidential Relationships (Reservation) Law (1995 Revision)". This law regards a breach of confidence towards a client as a criminal offence and suggests criminal penalties for offenders under the "Common Law".

Hence, confidential information in Cayman is considered sacrosanct and may not be disclosed to anyone, including a foreign government or a regulator who holds a foreign subpoena. The foreign government would have to proceed within the Cayman Islands court system in order to be able to receive privileged information. Service providers may only make disclosures to the client himself or to those who have express consent from the client to receive the information. A Cayman company is not required to make its register of directors and officers, its register of mortgages and charges, its shareholder register, or the mems & arts available to the public, unless a disclosure provision has been written into the mems & arts.

4.2.6   Marketing overseas

Last but not least, the fund will need another attribute to be marketable overseas: an ISIN number ("International Securities Identification Number"). An ISIN number is the international equivalent of the North American CUSIP ("Committee on Uniform Security Identification Procedures") number. It consists of nine characters straight. The ISIN number has a country code identifier as a prefix. Typically, the prefix contains two characters, but it can also contain three. In the case of the Cayman Islands, the prefix is three letters long. After the prefix follow nine digits which are finalized by a trailing "check digit" which is the tenth digit. ISIN numbers need to be applied for in the jurisdiction where the fund has been established. Most likely it will be the jurisdiction's central bank or a major exchange that is in charge with organizing or assigning the numbers for the securities. Every share class and series needs its own ISIN code. There are no ongoing fees to be paid for an ISIN number but only a one time fee at the time of establishment. Normally, the process of establishing an ISIN number is a quick one. This is partly due to the fact that the application for an ISIN number is probably the last item on the check list of the fund. Once a fund is ready to apply for an ISIN number, all other documentation has already been finalized. Therefore, everything the issuing office might ask for should be ready for submittal, no matter what.

Once the sponsor has been able to work out all of the previous details, he/she will be ready to attack the detailed process of establishing the offshore fund.

4.3   SETTING UP IN THE CAYMAN ISLANDS

There is a basic process for the setup of an offshore fund in each jurisdiction. Every domicile will use its own specific legal/regulatory terminology but the process in itself is fairly similar. Since the Cayman Islands are among the most popular chosen jurisdictions for the setup of alternative vehicles, I will describe the general setup process for an average Cayman Islands exempted company that will be registered as a mutual fund.[27]

Funds need to undergo an incorporation[28] process before they can be registered. Accordingly, the registration process is divided into two steps: the first step creates the entity, and the second step provides this entity with the right to function as an investment vehicle. In spite of that, because mutual funds are exempted companies they are not regulated by two different authorities as one might expect; the entity which has been formed as an exempted company is exempt from the Companies law but must be registered with the Registrar of Companies (the Registrar); the mutual fund, however, is regulated by the Mutual Funds Law under the authority of the Cayman Islands Monetary Authority (the CIMA).[29]

4.3.1   Registering with the registrar of companies

An exempted company is a corporation that fits section 182 of the Companies Law (2003 Revision), which says that all companies may apply for status as an exempted company, the objects of which are to be carried out mainly outside of the Cayman Islands. Usually, mutual funds trade on exchanges outside of the Islands,

---

[27]See Mutual Funds Law (2003 Revision) (2). Hedge funds in the Cayman Islands fall under the category of Mutual Funds and will be registered with the Cayman Islands Monetary Authority (CIMA) under the term "mutual funds".

[28]That is, if the choice has not been made to establish a trust instead of a company. Since trusts are no legal entities but contracts, they wouldn't need to incorporate. I choose to describe incorporation as an exempted company which is the process for most funds; however, it is also possible to incorporate a mutual fund as a partnership; companies are regulated under the Cayman Companies Law, and partnerships under the Partnership Law or the Exempted Limited Partnership Law; trusts are regulated under the Trust Law.

[29]www.cimoney.com.ky

and they sell their shares to buyers who are located outside of the Cayman Islands; thus, they fit the description and can be registered as exempted companies.[30]

The incorporation procedure is as follows:

(1) *Reserving the name of the new company.* Reserving a name for a new company allows the Registrar to investigate whether the name has not been used before by another company or whether the name contains restricted words. For example, a sponsor might choose to use the word "trust" in the name of the fund in order to imbue the fund with an aura of conservatism and dignity to help its marketing. This word could be a forbidden word for this fund, since "trust" carries several meanings one of which is a particular type of fund structure typically used in a conservative setting focused on preservation of capital without risk and connected to the services of professionals specialized in trusts.[31] Trusts and service providers who administer trusts must be licensed by the CIMA. Thus, a fund invoking the word "trust" in its name would suggest that it has gone through licensing by the CIMA as a bank and trust company which might not have been the case. Therefore, the law restricts the use of certain words within names.[32]

(2) *Paying an initial filing fee.* Each company must pay an initial filing fee the height of which depends on the size of the registered share capital of the company. A company that falls into the lowest category may register share capital of up to US$51,219 and must pay a filing fee of US$573.17.[33] The annual fee for the company payable in January of each year, will replicate the initial filing fee. This fee must be paid out to the "Cayman Islands Government" and be in the form of a CI$ or US$ check made out by a local bank. One cannot directly wire the money to the Registrar of Companies.

(3) *Delivering the mems & arts.* The memorandum and the articles of association (the "mems & arts") must be delivered in duplicate to the Registrar. The Registrar will then file and retain the original mems & arts and return the duplicate endorsed with a consecutive filing number and the date of registration, the "memorandum

---

[30]I am not trying to give legal advice. Each sponsor needs to consult his own lawyer in order to be certain that particular provisions apply to the fund he wants to structure.

[31]For trusts in the Cayman Islands refer to the informative article of Tompkins R.E. and Normandeau M. (1997) *"Maintaining the Quality of Offshore Trust Services in a Competitive Environment"*, Trusts, vol. 3 (Jan.) pp. 4–7.

[32]See Companies Law (2003 Revision) Section 30.; the following words are restricted: "Chamber of Commerce", "building society", "royal", "imperial", "empire", "municipal", "chartered", "co-operative", "assurance", "bank", "insurance", "administrator"; the company is not obliged to carry the words, Ltd., even if it is a limited liability company.

[33]Registered share capital exceeding US$51,219 but not exceeding US$999,998 requires an initial and annual fee of US$804.88; share capital exceeding US$ 999,998 but not exceeding US$1,999,996 requires US$1,687.79; share capital exceeding US$1,999,996 leads to an initial and annual fee of US$2,400 for the fund; all fees are subject to change.

of registration".[34] In addition, the Registrar issues a certificate of incorporation which is effective from the date of the registration of the memorandum.[35] The company must keep a "register of companies" that must contain the following information: (i) the name of the company; (ii) the address of the registered office of the fund; (iii) the share capital of the company, and if division into nominal and par value, then the number of shares into which it is divided and the fixed amounts thereof; (iv) the names and addresses of the subscribers to the memorandum and the share amount allocated to each of them; (v) the date of execution of the mems & arts; (vi) the filing date of the mems & arts; (vii) the number assigned to the company; (viii) and "in the case of a company limited by guarantee or which has no limit placed on the liability of its members, that the same is limited by guarantee or is unlimited, and if any of the particulars as hereinbefore specified are not pertinent to the applying company they may be omitted".[36] In case the mems & arts do not include the previous particulars, the register of companies must be annexed to the mems & arts.

(4) *Delivering the declaration according to section 184 of the Companies Law (2003 Revision).* As indicated above, Section 184 lays out the rules that must be followed by a company to qualify for exempted status. The sponsor or another subscriber of the fund will have to sign a declaration that confirms that the operations of the company will be mainly conducted outside of the Islands; and this declaration will need to be submitted to the Registrar. Indeed, this declaration will need to be deposited with the Registrar on an annual basis so that confirmation can be obtained by the Registrar that the location of the operations of the company still have not been transferred to the Cayman Islands. Once it becomes an annual routine this declaration is called the "annual return".[37]

Items (2)–(4) are typically all delivered simultaneously. Upon the filing of the Memorandum of Association by the Registrar, the company is deemed to be registered. Then, the fund will enter the next phase, which is the registration process with the CIMA.

4.3.2   Registration with the CIMA

The CIMA has developed application forms for funds[38] according to the section of the Mutual Funds Law (2003 Revision) for which the fund wants to be registered.

---

[34]See Companies Law (2003 Revision) Section 26 (1–2).
[35]See Companies Law (2003 Revision) Section 27 (1).
[36]See Companies Law (2003 Revision) Section 26 (3).
[37]See Companies Law (2003 Revision) Section 187.
[38]The Website address is: www.cimoney.com.ky; go to "Investments", then "application forms".

I am describing the requirements for a fund that wants to be registered under section 4(3)[39] of the Mutual Funds Law, a "registered" mutual fund. Registered mutual funds are the least regulated ones among the regulated mutual funds; and most hedge funds choose to write their offering documents such that they comply with section 4(3) of the Mutual Funds Law. The application form under section 4(3) developed by the CIMA is called the Form MF1. Based on its instructions, the following procedure must be followed: (1) submit the MF1 Form to the CIMA; (2) submit a Certified Copy of the Certificate of Incorporation/Registration issued by the Registrar; (3) submit prescribed registration fee; (4) in case certain items in the MF1 are answered by indicating the page numbers in which the topic is discussed within the offering document, submit a copy of the offering document; (5) submit the auditor's letter of consent; (6) submit the administrator's letter of consent; (7) and advise whether registered office or local administrator will be in charge of queries and fee payments:

(1) *Submit the MF1 Form to the CIMA.* The MF1 Form must be signed by the sponsor, the manager or the registered office on behalf of the mutual fund. The CIMA requires the fund to submit originals but it accepts faxed copies initially, as long as the original will be forwarded within 1 month of the registration.[40] The Form MF1 requests the fund to provide a synopsis of the offering document. The most relevant aspects of the information memorandum are covered in the MF1. The CIMA also accepts answers in the form that hint to the appropriate pages in the offering document. Therefore, the private placement memorandum (the PPM) typically accompanies the Form MF1 as an attachment.

(2) *Submit a Certified Copy of the Certificate of Incorporation issued by the Registrar.* A certified copy of incorporation can be obtained from the Registrar. For the most part, the fund will already have requested a certified copy from the Registrar at the time it received the original certificate.

(3) *Submit prescribed registration fee.* All categories of mutual funds pay the same in application and ongoing license renewal fees. Currently, this amount is US$2,439.02.[41]

(4) *Submit the offering document.* Usually, the law firm preparing the MF1 Form will also automatically attach a draft of the offering document to it, in case certain items in the MF1 are answered by indicating the page numbers in which the topic is discussed within. In spite of that it is not required by law to submit the information memorandum and the MF1 Form, it has become common practice to do so.

---

[39]These funds are considered "registered" funds.
[40]See MF1 Form, Notes (7).
[41]See CIMA website at www.cimoney.com.ky, go to "Publications", then " Fee Schedule". All fees are subject to change.

(5) *Submit the auditor's letter of consent*. The auditor's letter of consent must state that the audit firm has accepted the appointment as auditor for the fund. In addition, it must point out what accounting principles will be used and that it will fulfill its obligations under section 34 of the Mutual Funds Law.

Section 34 discusses the duties of an auditor of a regulated mutual fund towards the CIMA. The law requires the auditor to notify CIMA if there is any reason to believe that the fund might not be able to meet its obligations as they come to pass; or, if it appears that the fund conducts its business in a prejudicial way towards its creditors or investors; or if the fund manages its business without keeping proper accounting records so that its accounts could not be audited appropriately.[42]

(6) *Submit the administrator's letter of consent*. The administrator's letter of consent must indicate its acceptance of the appointment for the fund. The administrator must summarize the type of services he will provide for the fund and sign that he has reviewed the fund documentation before the MF1 has been submitted. By signing a letter of consent, the administrator acknowledges that all of the fund's promoters and service providers have passed the due diligence process.[43]

While some funds might be exempted by the CIMA from having an administrator, it would be highly unusual for a fund to be exempted by the CIMA from appointing an auditor. Currently, all regulated funds must have an auditor who will perform an annual audit based on the financial year of the fund.

(7) *Advise whether registered office or local administrator will be in charge of queries and fee payments*. Before the CIMA agrees to register a fund it wants to make sure that the fund will pay its fees on time. Thus, it needs an address and a company/individual who will take responsibility for paying the annual fees for the fund and who will be available in case the CIMA has any queries about the vehicle. Usually, these tasks are provided by the "registered office"[44] of the fund or by its administrator. Thus, the fund needs to address these issues in its application materials submitted with the CIMA.

---

[42]If an auditor violates this provision, he will be fined US$24,390.20. Mutual Funds Law (2003 Revision), 34(1).

[43]According to the Mutual Funds Law (2003 Revision), Section 16, a mutual fund administrator must satisfy itself that each promoter of the fund is of sound reputation, that the administration of the fund will be undertaken by service providers who have expertise in their area of service and are of sound reputation, and that the business of the fund and any offer of equity interest in it will be carried out in a proper way. If the administrator does not follow this provision, he can be fined US$121,951 for this transgression.

[44]The rule for every company to hold a "registered office" can be found in the Companies Law (2003 Revision), 50. It is a regulation which protects the creditors of the company; all communication and notices should be addressed to the registered office of the company. Most of the times it is the administrator who will provide the registered office to the fund but it can also be a corporate services provider.

After CIMA has reviewed the application materials, the fund will receive a "Mutual Fund Registration" which includes the "license" number of the fund. Funds will thus receive a "License Number" in spite of that in most cases they will not fall under the category "licensed"[45] but "registered"[46] funds; however, all of them will be "regulated mutual funds".[47] At this point the fund is considered registered and it can start conducting its business.

4.3.3   Timeline and application for tax exemption

Both processes together have a timeline of less than two weeks. The company can be set up within 24 hours by payment of an express fee[48] or within three days if regular procedures are followed. Fund registration will take CIMA between 2 – 5 business days. Thus, if everything works smoothly it is not impossible for a Cayman offshore fund to be established within a week.

In addition to incorporation and registration, the company (fund) will apply for the tax exemption certificate. The application process is fairly simple. A certified copy of the certificate of incorporation needs to be sent to the "Glass House"[49] where the Governor in Executive Council resides. The application must be accompanied by a fee of US$183 and the company will receive[50] a so-called "undertaking" within approximately 3 weeks from the date of submission. The tax exemption will establish that for a period of 20 years from the date of the undertaking, the fund cannot be imposed with any taxes on profits, gains, income, or appreciation. In addition, no taxes in the nature of estate duty or inheritance tax can be laid upon the fund. The Tax Exemption Certificate is issued by the Governor in executive council under the Tax Concessions Law. Of course there exists a similar provision for exempted trusts in the Trusts Law.

4.3.4   Signing offshore while being onshore

In practice, the application process and the obtaining of the Tax Exemption Certificate is fully instigated and completed by the offshore law firm hired by the

---

[45]See Mutual Funds Law (2003 Revision) (4)(1)(a).

[46]Andrew Murray: "Regulation of Mutual Funds in the Cayman Islands" in: International Offshore and Financial Centres Handbook, 1999/2000.

[47]See Mutual Funds Law (2003 Revision) Section 2.

[48]According to the Companies Law (2003 Revision) (220), the Registrar will expedite the formation of a company if such company pays an additional fee of US$487.80. If the complete application package is received before 12 pm (noon) on a working day, there will be same day processing and the company will be registered at the end of the working day; if the application is received after 12 pm on a working day, the company will be registered by 12pm (noon) the following working day.

[49]Government Administration Building, Elgin Avenue, George Town, Grand Cayman.

[50]Whoever has applied for the "undertaking" will also receive it. Hence, if the law firm applies for it, it will be sent to the law firm, if the registered office has applied for it, it will be sent to the registered office of the company.

fund. In order to be able to comply with the various signing requirements, law firms will provide interim directors for the fund through their affiliated companies or directly. The law firm will also be the initial shareholder of the fund. In due time but surely before the fund starts operation, the law firm will enact a share transfer to the actual shareholders of the fund and the interim directors will resign for the benefit of the permanent directors. All of these corporate actions will have been documented in the first minutes of the fund and by various resolutions confirming the appointed directors and officers. These documents constitute the first part of the minutes book of the fund. Whoever will be in charge of the registered office will also need to maintain the minutes book.

All practical requirements have been fulfilled at this point, and the procedures are as good as completed. The fund may start trading. However, there is one aspect which I would like to introduce in some more detail to the fund sponsor so that he/she might get an opportunity to ponder it for his/her offshore venture in Cayman: the Segregated Portfolio Company (SPC).

4.3.5   Choosing a company structure – the SPC

A fund manager might decide to take the opportunity and set up his/her fund in the newest most innovative shape of Cayman company structures: the SPC.

The SPC is a much improved version of the previous "umbrella fund". An umbrella fund was formed by establishing a Cayman Islands exempted company with several classes of redeemable shares, whereby each class could represent a completely different portfolio of assets. However, umbrella structures encountered problems connected to the rights of their creditors. The different classes of redeemable shares with dissimilar investment styles were not ring fenced against each other. This meant that since the fund is a single legal entity separate from its shareholders and directors the rights of creditors counted against the company itself as a whole, and creditors were able to enforce their claims against any of the company's assets.[51] Even if the mems & arts of the umbrella company had been drafted such that the directors were required to maintain separate accounts in respect of the assets and liabilities attributable to each separate class of shares with a dissimilar investment style, these provisions might not have held in court had creditors ascertained their rights versus the company.

Since the umbrella fund structure had been the structure of choice for many hedge funds in the past, it had become evident to Cayman authorities that there was a gap in the legal landscape of company structures in relation to funds. Consequently, they had

---

[51]There is no provision in the Companies Law for "umbrella" structures.

to find regulations that better served the protection of fund of funds investors. The development of the SPC legislation in 2002 is the Cayman attempt to mend this gap.

An SPC may establish one or more segregated portfolios (SPs). These are separate portfolios which may have completely different investment styles and which segregate the assets and liabilities attributable to each SP from the assets and liabilities attributable to every other SP and from the general assets and liabilities of the Company.[52] Only the SPC is the legal entity, however, each SP must be separately designated and the SPC must file an annual notice specifying the name of each SP it has created.[53] The SPC may enter into contracts and transactions for all or specific SPs whereby the names of the affected SPs have to be listed.

The directors of an SPC must establish and maintain the segregation of the SP assets from the general assets of the company. As of January 2003, directors of the SPC who fail to satisfy this requirement, incur personal liability.[54] Only the Grand Court of the Cayman Islands may relieve the directors from this liability in certain circumstances. It is important to protect the general assets of the company from a "flow over" of an SP by including a prohibition of such a flow over into the Articles of Association of the SPC.[55]

In order to enforce any of the above it is considered prudent to have all contracts regarding the SPC governed by Cayman Islands law and to select Cayman courts as having jurisdiction in case of a dispute. While Delaware, Guernsey and Bermuda[56] have been introduced to the statutory concept of the segregation of assets in a limited liability company for a couple of years, other jurisdictions will need to develop a familiarity with it before its proper enforcement can be implied.

For a fund to be registered as an SPC, first it needs to acquire written consent from the CIMA.[57] This changes the application process as to what I had described before in such as that the fund first needs to submit a draft of the offering document to the CIMA, the CIMA will then provide a written consent for the Registrar of Companies so that the company may be incorporated as an SPC. There are no additional fees payable to the CIMA for the written consent. The fees for incorporation as an SPC to the Registrar of Companies include at least an additional US$609.75 initial application fee for a company whose authorized share capital doesn't exceed

---

[52]See Companies Law (2003 Revision) (240–242).

[53]See Companies Law (2003 Revision) (233) (6).

[54]See Companies Law (2003 Revision) (238) (2).

[55]See Companies Law (2003 Revision) (241) (1) (a) (ii).

[56]Bermuda had passed the "Segregated Accounts Companies Amendment Act 2002" which allows funds to be established in the form of "Segregated Account Companies" (SAC). The SAC is the Bermuda counterpart to the Cayman SPC; the Guernsey counterpart of the SPC is called PCC which stands for "Protected Cell Company" and is governed by the "Protected Cell Companies (Special Purpose Vehicle) Regulations, 2001; Jersey anticipates to introduce a PCC by the end of 2004.

[57]Companies Law (2003 Revision) (234) (1) (c).

US$50,000. Ongoing fees for an SPC are also higher than the comparable fees for an exempted company. There is an annual fee of US$2,439.02 payable each January plus an additional annual SPC fee for each existing SP of US$365.85 with a cap at US$1,829.27.

Funds can use the SPC structure for all types of purposes. For example, it is entirely possible to structure a fund that has one SP structured in the form of a bond, and another one in the form of income notes, thereby satisfying the tax needs as they might appear in various countries.

The SPC is a good example for Cayman's flexibility and speed in creating a legal framework for a dominant industry. It provides ample proof that hedge funds don't only follow their herd instinct but know very well which infrastructure suits them best when they seem to give preference to certain jurisdictions over others.

There is a lot more to say about starting and maintaining offshore funds in various jurisdictions.

Ideally, this chapter would now close with a comparison of all offshore jurisdictions currently "in fashion" for hedge funds. However, the topic would require a book itself and will need to be discussed another time. As has been shown, going offshore is not a simple matter but it can be both financially and professionally rewarding to do so. A sponsor who gives thought to all considerations previously discussed should be in excellent shape to start an offshore fund. His preparation will guarantee success for the project. Unlike the nightmare stories experienced by plenty of other promoters, the prepared sponsor will harvest the fruit of his proper planning: reduced overall costs and a happy client.

4.4   LIST OF REFERENCES AND READINGS

Alternative Funds Service Review. (2003). *Cayman 2003 Report*. London, UK.

Andersen, E. (2003). *"Memorandum on the Netherlands Antilles Exempt Company"*, SS&C Fund Services N.V., Curacao.

Appleby, Spurling, and Kempe. (2003). *Cayman Islands International Business Guide*. 2003 Edition. ISI Publications Limited.

Appleby, Spurling, and Kempe. (2003). *Setting up Funds Offshore*. The AS&K Guide to Key Offshore Centres. Incisive media, London.

Bermuda Monetary Authority Quarterly Update. Nov. 2003, passim.

Bethel, R.G. (2003). *"Transparency & Information Exchange"*. Government of the Bahamas, Bahamas Financial Services Board, Sept. 25.

Cayman Islands Monetary Authority. (2003). *Guidance Notes on the Prevention and Detection of Money Laundering in the Cayman Islands*. Cayman Islands.

Cayman Islands Monetary Authority. http://www.cimoney.com.ky

Chadwick, R. (2004). E-Mail Conversations, Financial Services Commission, British Virgin Islands.

Cleare, E. (2004). Telephone Conversation, Securities Commission of the Bahamas, (March 26).

Ferreira, F.P. "The Protected Cell Companies in a Nutshell". http://www.legalinfo-panama.com/articulos/articulos_41a.htm.

http://www.bfsb-bahamas.com

http://www.scb.gov.bs. Homepage of The Securities Commission of the Bahamas.

Hurst, M.A. (2003). "Offshore Jurisdictions: Choices, Challenges and Changes", Presentation at the Wealth Management Forum 2003, Geneva, Switzerland. Nov. 13.

Mortishead, C. (2003). *"Messy European tax laws provoke the Cayman people"*. Nov. 26. https://www.timesonline.co.uk/article/0"630-908182,00.html

Murray, A. (1999/2000). "Regulation of Mutual Funds in the Cayman Islands", International Offshore and Financial Centres Handbook.

Standards Helpfile 13. https://standards.fundserv.com/english/helpfile13/data_standards/d_cusip_isin_num.htm

The Companies Law, (2003 Revision). Cayman Islands Government.

The Investment Funds Regulations. (2003). The Investment Funds Act (No. 20 of 2003). Draft. Bahamas Government.

The Mutual Funds Act. (1995). The Bahamas Government.

The Mutual Funds Law, (2003 Revision). Cayman Islands Government.

Tompkins, R.E. and Normandeau, M. (1997). "Maintaining the Quality of Offshore Trust Services in a Competitive Environment". Trusts & Trustees, Vol. 3 (Jan) pp. 4–7.

Chapter 5

Structured products on hedge funds

JEAN-MARIE BARREAU AND JAESON DUBROVAY

5.1 THE BASICS

Investors can benefit substantially by adding hedge fund strategies to their portfolios due to their diversification properties and absolute return objectives. Structured Products (SPs) on hedge funds evolved to serve the needs of a significant constituency of investors who were unable or unwilling to invest in hedge funds in the formats in which they were offered. The advantages of SPs over conventional hedge fund investments are that SPs can offer enhancements such as superior risk management, enhanced (more frequent) liquidity, access to leverage and/or principal protection.

These products can be thought of as having three distinct components: the underlying hedge fund asset (Hedge Fund Asset), the payout and the wrapper. The Hedge Fund Asset is either a fund of hedge funds or an index tied to a basket of hedge funds. The payout formula determines how the value of a product at maturity relates to the Hedge Fund Asset. In tracker products (discussed later), the payout is linked one-to-one with the Hedge Fund Asset while in principal-protected structures, the initial capital invested is guaranteed at maturity. The wrapper is the "packaging" of the SP, which may impact the tax and/or regulatory treatment of the product. The most commonly used wrappers are notes, swaps and options, each one providing investors with a custom-tailored solution for access to the Hedge Fund Asset.

One of the most difficult problems facing the providers (Providers) of SPs linked to hedge funds is the lack of transparency and liquidity associated with investing in Hedge Fund Assets. The most effective solution to this problem is to establish separately managed accounts (Managed Accounts) with each manager that are segregated and managed in a manner similar to the manager's flagship fund. This gives the Providers of the SP a much higher level of comfort in terms of transparency, risk monitoring and liquidity.

5.2 EVOLUTION OF STRUCTURED PRODUCTS

Structured notes have been in existence since the 1980s with the first ones initially linked to a basket of commodity trading advisors. A zero coupon bond (ZCB), purchased at a discount, was used to guarantee the initial principal at maturity, while the balance was invested in Managed Accounts with selected commodity trading advisors. The trading advisors were able to gain exposure to the markets equal to 100% of the amount of the investor's initial principal since commodity investments only require a small margin deposit to trade. As the markets evolved and investors demanded access to hedge funds, structured notes were created using the same ZCB structure. Since these products could not avail themselves of the inherent leverage in commodities because they invested directly in hedge funds, only a small amount was available for investment in the Hedge Fund Asset. This structure generated returns that were unsatisfactory overall since only a small portion of an investor's total investment was exposed to the markets.

One alternative to increase the level of investment in the Hedge Fund Asset was to replicate the value of the ZCB through a "zero coupon swap, backed by a letter of credit". This construct allows two parties to exchange fixed-for-floating rate payments without having to put up the notional amount, which is collateralized by a letter of credit as opposed to securities. In this case, since the ZCB was not actually purchased, investors were able to increase their participation in the Hedge Fund Asset to 100%. At inception, a floating "stop loss level" was established based on the mark-to-market value of the ZCB (with a similar maturity as the SP) and performance of the Hedge Fund Asset was monitored daily. If the performance of the Hedge Fund Asset became negative to the point of approaching the floating "stop loss level", then exposure to the Hedge Fund Asset was reduced to zero, the guarantor bought a ZCB for the balance of the term and investors had to wait until maturity to get back their original investment.

These shortcomings drove the development of options-based SPs, making it possible to give investors 100% exposure to the Hedge Fund Asset, even if the investments were made directly into individual hedge funds. The options-based SPs invest a large portion of the initial capital in a ZCB to secure the original investment, and use the balance to buy a custom-tailored option on the Hedge Fund Asset. At maturity, the option payout tracks the movement of the Hedge Fund Asset on a dollar-for-dollar basis. In the case where the option value is zero, investors recoup their initial investment. It is common for SPs to be sold as medium-term notes for a variety of economic, structural and regulatory reasons. Through their structure and payout mechanisms, SPs give the investor a meaningful participation in the Hedge Fund Asset, access to leverage and/or principal protection.

As a result of these innovative products, the hedge fund industry is attracting assets from investors who want the diversification and absolute return benefits from hedge fund investing, but have little or no experience with hedge funds or are sensitive to loss of principal. High net worth (HNW) investors are increasingly being targeted by distributors, while institutions with a low appetite for risk are showing great interest in SPs provided by institutions with strong credit ratings from recognized agencies. These investors prefer products that provide principal protection, which transfers some of the risks associated with hedge funds from the investor to the Provider of the product. At the same time, many hedge funds have become more transparent in the way they conduct business, which has increased the level of comfort in products linked to them. Together, these trends have fueled the massive growth of interest in SPs that has added to the recent growth of the hedge fund industry.

5.3   TYPES OF STRUCTURED PRODUCTS

The most common types of SPs are designed to track, leverage and/or provide principal protection to a Hedge Fund Asset such as a hedge fund index or a fund of hedge funds. Trackers usually provide the same return as the Hedge Fund Asset but typically have additional features, such as denomination in a specific currency and/or listing on a stock exchange. Leveraged products such as swaps, forwards and options, allow investors to expose a multiple of their initial investment (typically 2–5 times) to the Hedge Fund Asset as well as having potential tax or regulatory advantages. There are two commonly used methods of creating principal protection products: the static structure, often referred to as "bond plus call option" and the dynamic structure, more frequently referred to as "constant proportion portfolio insurance" (CPPI). An underappreciated advantage of SPs is that their flexibility allows the basic construction to be modified to accommodate the specific needs of a particular investor and that they are constantly improving through ongoing financial engineering innovations. These products are described in more detail below.

5.3.1   Tracker products

Tracker products, sometimes referred to as "Delta one" or "pass-through" products, are viewed as an alternative to a direct investment in Hedge Fund Assets. They are intended to provide investors with 100% upside and downside participation in the performance of the Hedge Fund Asset. Such products are usually issued as "access products" and are designed to overcome the hurdles that many investors face when investing directly in hedge funds. These hurdles vary from jurisdiction to jurisdiction, but some of the issues more commonly encountered by investors are:

- Most hedge funds are US dollar denominated, involving potential currency risk for investors whose home currency is not the US dollar.
- There is unfavourable tax treatment of direct investments in offshore funds for domestic investors in many jurisdictions (including the United Kingdom, the United States and Germany).
- Most hedge funds are offshore and unregulated, and therefore not easily accessible to a wide range of investors.

- Only limited information about hedge funds is available publicly, making an informed investment decision difficult. Hedge fund investments require careful selection and ongoing monitoring of managers, strategies and performance, which is almost impossible without an experienced investment advisor as a partner in the investment process.
- Unlike traditional investment funds, hedge funds cannot be bought and sold on a daily basis. Each hedge fund has specific terms dictating how and when investments can be made or redeemed. In addition, they often require lengthy lockup periods and a considerable notice period prior to redemption.
- Proceeds from the redemption of hedge fund investments are usually paid out only quarterly or annually, resulting in substantially lower liquidity than traditional assets. One of the reasons for this is that hedge funds often take sophisticated positions, or make investments in illiquid instruments, many of which require significant lengths of time to deliver the expected results.

Tracker products typically have the same return profile as direct hedge fund investments, but they also tend to have additional features that are designed to address some of the issues described above:

- The returns of the underlying Hedge Fund Asset may be hedged into a currency of choice.
- The products may be wrapped as index certificates, insurance policies, etc., which in many cases enables the investors to enjoy a more favourable fiscal or regulatory treatment.
- The products may be registered for public distribution in specific onshore jurisdictions.
- The Hedge Fund Assets may be managed by a reputable and experienced investment advisor.
- Tracker products are usually issued as securitized derivatives, and are often listed on one or several stock exchanges. This makes it possible for investors to trade them like a stock or a bond, usually with monthly, weekly or even daily liquidity.
- If the product is issued as a securitized derivative, trades are usually settled within a few days via a clearing agent.

The Hedge Fund Asset for a tracker product is usually either a hedge fund index or a diversified portfolio of hedge funds. Exposure to a single hedge fund, or to a small basket of hedge funds is less common due to the higher specific risk associated with such a concentrated exposure.

Tracker products targeting the HNW segment of the market are usually issued as securitized derivatives, rather than as over-the-counter derivatives, and are frequently listed on a stock exchange. Securitized trackers often appeal to a wider universe of investors as they can be registered for public distribution in specific jurisdictions and listed on a stock exchange, which improves liquidity.

5.3.2   Leveraged structures

There are two commonly used structures for providing investors with leveraged exposure to Hedge Fund Assets, regardless of whether they are a single hedge fund, an index or a fund of hedge funds.

The first of these is the option type structure, where the payout is based on the value of the Hedge Fund Asset at maturity. In this type of structure, the participation in the Hedge Fund Asset is static, meaning that the degree of leverage will fall as the value of the Hedge Fund Asset rises.

The second type of structure, used for certificates, notes and swaps, is a dynamic structure, meaning that the amount of borrowing is adjusted on a regular basis depending on the performance of the Hedge Fund Asset. Dynamic leveraging features allow the amount of borrowing to increase when the value of the Hedge Fund Asset rises, and to be reduced when the Hedge Fund Asset value falls. This ensures that the leverage remains essentially proportional throughout the life of the product. Leveraged products are used by sophisticated investors (HNW individuals, family offices and funds of hedge funds) either to target improved returns or to secure a favourable tax treatment via the payout modification.

5.3.3   Principal protection structures

There are two commonly used methods for creating principal protected products: the static structure, often referred to "bond plus call option", and the dynamic structure, more frequently referred to as "constant proportion portfolio insurance" or CPPI.

Products employing the static structure are designed such that the principal protection is achieved by combining two elements. One delivers the principal protection at maturity, and is usually a ZCB, while the other provides the Hedge Fund Asset exposure, and is usually a derivative or an equity instrument. Products that use a dynamic structure do not buy the principal protection at inception; instead they achieve it by constantly rebalancing between the risk-free asset (Bond Pool) and the risky underlying Hedge Fund Asset.

Static structures (*bond plus call option*)

This construction assumes that the Provider will invest a portion of the proceeds of the issue in a note, often an ZCB with a matching maturity date as the SP Note. The remaining assets are used to buy an instrument providing the Hedge Fund Asset exposure; usually in the form of an option. At issuance, the amount reserved for the ZCB is the amount which, at maturity, will have a value equal to 100% of the initial investment. This amount will therefore depend on the level of interest rates at inception and the maturity date of the ZCB. Generally, lower interest rate levels and shorter maturities mean that a greater portion of the issue proceeds must be allocated to the ZCB.

There are three chief disadvantages to static structures. First, low interest rate levels mean that a high proportion of the assets will be consumed by the ZCB. Second, options on hedge funds are priced at a very high implied volatility when compared with their historical volatility data, which means that they tend to be expensive. As a result, this type of structure currently tends to either have a low participation rate in the Hedge Fund Asset or a long maturity, which explains the number of products on offer with maturities in excess of 10 years. The final disadvantage of this structure is that the Provider will initially invest a substantially lower percentage of the proceeds from the investor in the Hedge Fund Asset.

The main advantage of the static structure is that it is transparent and easy to comprehend. Since the participation rate in the Hedge Fund Asset is fixed at inception, it is easy to model the payout based on the return expectations of the Hedge Fund Asset. This approach has been very popular with distribution channels aimed at HNW investors. The current low interest rate levels, however, have increasingly shifted emphasis towards dynamic structures.

Dynamic structures (CPPI)

This structure was designed so investors can avoid having to pay up front for the principal protection in the form of an ZCB as they do in static structures. As we noted earlier, this is particularly beneficial for investments in hedge funds, where the implied volatility used to price the option component is usually expensive. In dynamic structures, the assets of the product are constantly reallocated between two asset pools: the risky Hedge Fund Asset and a risk-free Bond Pool. The allocation to each asset is adjusted on a regular basis by measuring the difference between the ongoing net asset value (NAV), which includes the value of the Hedge Fund Asset and the value of the Bond Pool, and its so-called reference level (RL) (i.e. the price of a notional ZCB). Clearly, as the NAV approaches the RL, most of the assets will be re-allocated to the Bond Pool (Figure 1).

The percentage invested in the Hedge Fund Asset is referred to as the "Investment Level" and is determined by the following formula:

$$\text{Investment Level} = \frac{(\text{NAV}-\text{RL}) \times \text{Multiplier}}{\text{NAV}} \times 100$$

The Multiplier is a constant factor that is determined at inception to ensure that the initial Investment Level of the product is equal to 100%. It is because of the Multiplier that this type of structure is referred to as CPPI.

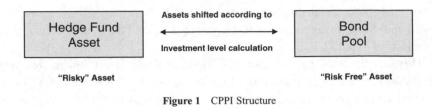

"Risky" Asset   "Risk Free" Asset

Figure 1   CPPI Structure

Example where RL is fixed at inception

In the following example, the issue price and initial NAV of the product are both 100; the RL is fixed at 80 at inception and 100 at maturity, the difference providing an initial buffer (Cushion) of 20; the maturity is 5 years, and the Multiplier has been set at 5 in order to give an Investment Level of 100% at inception (see below). The Multiplier was derived as (100% Investment Level/Cushion) = 5. The calculations below are made without any allowance for fees or costs associated with the structure (Figure 2).

At inception

$$(\text{Month 1}) \text{ Investment Level} = \text{Cushion} \times \text{Multiplier}$$

$$100\% = 20\% \times 5$$

End of month 1

Assume the Hedge Fund Asset has fallen in value by 0.5% and that the RL is now 80.3 (20% cushion amortized over 60 months = 0.33% per month appreciation in RL), the new Investment Level for Month 2 will be calculated as follows:

$$(\text{Month 2}) \text{ Investment Level} = \frac{(99.5 - 80.3)}{99.5} \times 5 \times 100 = 96.5\%$$

As a result of the recalculation, 3.5% of the exposure to the Hedge Fund Asset is transferred to the Bond Pool at the end of the month (Figure 3).

End of month 2

Assume the Hedge Fund Asset increases by 4.5%, the Bond Pool earns an annualized 5% and that the RL has increased by another 0.33% to 80.7. The new NAV is calculated as the Hedge Fund Asset value (96.5 × 1.045) plus the Bond Pool value [(3.5 × 1.05)/12] = 101.1. The Investment Level for month 3 is calculated as follows (Figure 4)

$$(\text{Month 3}) \text{ Investment Level} = \frac{(101.1 - 80.7)}{101.1} \times 5 \times 100 = 101.0\%$$

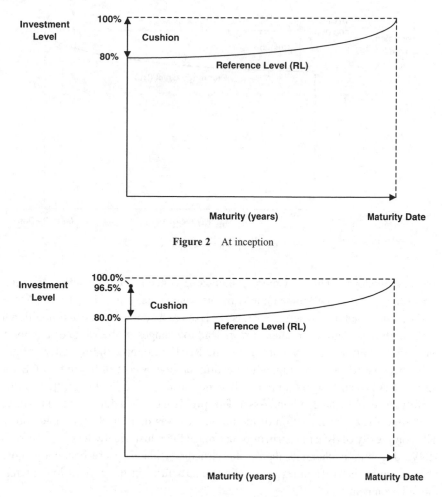

Figure 2 At inception

Figure 3 End of month 1

As a result, the exposure to the Hedge Fund Asset will increase at the end of month 2 and, assuming that the Investment Level is not capped at 100%, the SP will have a leveraged exposure to the Hedge Fund Asset for month 3. The leverage is typically made available by the SP Provider through their treasury operations.

The true cost of a CPPI product depends on four key factors: the volatility of the Hedge Fund Asset; the size of the Multiplier; the value of the RL (which may be dependent on interest rates); and the frequency of re-balancing. Since CPPI structures work best with low volatility Hedge Fund Assets, they have been applied more successfully to hedge fund-based products than to traditional equity-based products.

The chief disadvantage of dynamic structures is that the payout is "path-dependent", i.e. it depends on the performance of the Hedge Fund Asset which affects the

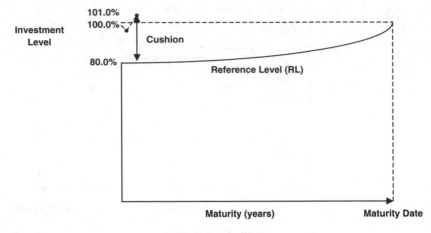

Figure 4   End of month 2

leverage employed. This is a more complicated concept than the static structure, where the payout is determined purely by the final value of the Hedge Fund Asset.

Dynamic structures, where the RL is *not* fixed at inception, can cause additional complexities as changes in interest rates lead to changes in the value of the bond, which in turn affects the level of the floating RL. For example, falling interest rates will cause the RL to move higher (reflecting the higher cost of buying a ZCB for protection), which triggers a higher allocation to the Bond Pool regardless of the performance of the Hedge Fund Asset. This problem can be addressed by Providers fixing the RL at the inception of the product as was done in the example above. The complexity of dynamic structures has made them historically less popular with HNW distribution channels than static structures, but they are becoming more popular given the difficulties of using static structures in the current low interest rate environment.

Principal protected-structures have proven to be popular with HNW investors, particularly in Europe, the Middle East and Asia, but some institutional investors have sought principal-protected structures for regulatory reasons. For institutional investors, it may make sense to explore some of the more recent innovative payout structures, which can be both cheaper and easier to price than traditional fixed-maturity principal protected structures.

5.4   USING STRUCTURED PRODUCTS

Investors derive a number of benefits from using SPs, depending on their circumstances. SPs have been used regularly for leveraged access to hedge funds and/or tax efficiency for HNW investors, but they have also been used by institutional investors to improve their capital ratios.

Hedge fund managers wishing to grow their investor base may find that potential investors with particular regulatory or tax issues can invest more advantageously through an SP vehicle. Hedge fund managers interested in pursuing this channel should be aware that there are a number of advantages as well as clear disadvantages.

The primary issue is the liquidity requirements of both the investor and the Provider of the SP. Most investors typically require at least monthly liquidity, while the Provider may require more frequent liquidity in the underlying funds in order to adjust hedges. This means that strategies employing liquid assets are more suitable for SPs than illiquid strategies, for two reasons. First, the Provider wishes to ensure that the liquidity requirements do not hamper the manager's ability to carry out his investment strategy. Second, the hedge fund manager wants to ensure that the liquidity requirements of the Provider and investors do not unfavourably impact other investors in his hedge funds. This is particularly important for leveraged products or principal-protected products with high multipliers. For example, if the multiplier is set at 5, a drawdown of 5.0% in the Hedge Fund Asset will reduce the exposure to the Hedge Fund Asset by about 25%.

Another issue is transparency, since most Providers need to actively monitor their exposure to the Hedge Fund Asset. The information they require normally includes a daily estimate of the Hedge Fund Asset's NAV, but they will typically also need to monitor the portfolio against a pre-established investment policy (IP) and perform analytical risk management techniques on the underlying securities. The IP typically covers the amount of leverage that may be employed and the liquidity and diversification of the assets in the Managed Account. The IP is usually based on the manager's own internal investment guidelines so as to minimize the divergence of performance between the manager's flagship fund and the Managed Account. The Managed Account is monitored by the Provider using advanced risk management tools.

Another important issue is that of the volatility of the Hedge Fund Asset. As we noted earlier, dynamic structures are more expensive for investors when the volatility of the Hedge Fund Asset is high. Outcome analysis of CPPI structures suggests that an expected annualized volatility of more than 12–15% significantly increases the probability of the product returning no more than the initial principal.

5.5 KEY VALUE DRIVERS

Creating SPs is an evolutionary process that allows innovators to develop products as they perceive demand from investors. Investors in SPs need to understand and evaluate several key value drivers that will impact the usefulness and quality of SPs as a solution to their specific needs.

5.5.1   Underlying fund

The structure and management of the Hedge Fund Asset is very important as these characteristics permeate all aspects of the product. Hedge Fund Assets can track either a passive hedge fund index or an actively managed fund of hedge funds. Since individual hedge fund strategies tend to have periods when they are in favour and other periods when they underperform, active management can add meaningful value by identifying and emphasizing the more attractive strategies while still retaining prudent diversification. Understanding the various product structures, the universe of strategies and how each individual manager executes his specific strategy is a full time endeavour. It is imperative for investors to work with an investement advisor that has the experience and ability to successfully structure the product, select appropriate managers, monitor and revise asset allocation, and perform sophisticated ongoing risk management.

In general terms, a Hedge Fund Asset that is concentrated is expected to have higher volatility than one that is well diversified. Higher volatility in a Hedge Fund Asset has several drawbacks such as higher structuring costs and more frequent drawdowns (consecutive periods that experience losses). Since option pricing is highly dependent on the volatility of the Hedge Fund Asset, a less volatile fund will generally be less expensive to structure. In addition, pronounced frequent drawdowns can cause the systematic asset allocation model to deleverage the investment away from the Hedge Fund Asset in favour of the Bond Pool, which will dilute overall exposure to the Hedge Fund Asset thus negatively impacting overall returns.

In cases where the SPs employ dynamic leveraging, a volatile Hedge Fund Asset will expose the product to the negative aspects of this structure. Dynamic leveraging is beneficial because it typically increases exposure to the Hedge Fund Asset when the NAV is rising (aggressive), and deleverages when the Hedge Fund Asset experiences losses (defensive). If the losses continue over several periods, the fund may in fact deleverage itself to a point well below the initial participation rate of 100%. In the case of a volatile fund, losses will tend to occur when leverage is highest, while gains will typically occur when the fund is underexposed to the Hedge Fund Asset.

Investors in SPs should also be aware that funds can be structured in a multitude of ways to address their specific needs. An example would be where the product has 100% exposure to the Hedge Fund Asset, yet the investor's return from the Hedge Fund Asset is capped at a fraction of his exposure (e.g. 80%–90%) in an effort to reduce stated fees. While the gross Hedge Fund Asset returns may be attractive, the capped exposure effectively reduces the overall rate of return on the SP. The gains above the capped exposure inure to the SP Provider.

5.5.2 Liquidity

There are a variety of methods to provide liquidity, most of which depend on the product structure and method used to provide the exposure to the Hedge Fund Asset. The key driver of liquidity is whether the investment is made via an index, a Managed Account or directly into a hedge fund. Investments made via index or Managed Accounts generally offer more frequent liquidity, while investments made directly into hedge funds restrict investors to the redemption policy stated in the fund's offering memorandum. In some cases, managers may issue side-letters that permit more frequent redemptions, but these are only as good as the liquidity of the underlying securities in which the hedge fund invests and the manager's disposition towards honouring the side-letters. In addition, investors will typically want to redeem from a manager when the manager is least inclined to accept redemptions due to illiquidity, strategy pressure and/or portfolio structure reasons. Redemption side-letters generally provide illusory tangible benefits in managing the liquidity of direct investments in hedge funds.

Managed Accounts allow separation of the Hedge Fund Assets from the manager as he acts only in an investment advisor capacity to the Managed Account. As a result, the Provider has complete control of the Managed Account, which not only allows risk management techniques to be employed at the security level, but more importantly, it allows the Provider to dictate the ultimate liquidity of the investment, if necessary. This is extremely valuable in cases where a hedge fund comes under pressure and the manager elects to suspend redemptions. In this extreme case, the Managed Account can be liquidated immediately without experiencing the magnitude of loss or impairment of liquidity by otherwise investing directly in his hedge fund.

The maturity term of an SP is based on interest rates in effect at the time of the offering. Higher interest rates generally translate into fewer years to maturity, while lower interest rates dictate a longer maturity. While hedge fund investments require a medium-term investment horizon, investors may want access to their funds within a reasonable period of time should their liquidity circumstances change unexpectedly. It is important for investors to determine the frequency with which redemptions in specific products are allowed and whether any costs are associated with exercising their redemption privilege.

5.5.3 Risk management

The degree of control over risk is typically determined by how the investment is made with each specific hedge fund manager. When investing directly in hedge funds, an investor may have frequent contact with the manager who will explain the strategy currently employed in the fund and other relevant information about the fund. There are degrees of transparency with each manager, depending on variables such as the perceived ease of replication of the manager's strategy, the degree of proprietary value of his investment process and structural issues such as disclosing short positions and\or partial long positions that are in the process of being fully established. The ability to accurately evaluate risks in the portfolio, and take corrective action should problems arise, is diluted when investments are made directly into hedge funds.

In contrast, investments made via Managed Accounts provide useful information at the security level upon which risk analysis techniques can be applied. This risk analysis can result in a more realistic evaluation of risks in the portfolio such as exposing breaches of position limits and/or sector exposure constraints and real-time evaluation of pre-established portfolio liquidity measures. Value-at-Risk analysis and stress testing is also rendered more robust with access to each underlying security in a manager's portfolio.

5.5.4   Product structure

The quality of the SP guarantor, as established by recognized rating agencies, is of utmost importance in placing a value on the quality of the structure. The higher the quality of the guarantor, the higher the likelihood that the guarantee will have substance should the guarantor need to carry out his contractual obligations. In addition, since the quality ascribed to the guarantor directly affects his cost of financing and indirectly affects an investor's cost of leverage, higher credit ratings generally mean lower financing costs to investors and, as a result, more attractive rates of return.

Fees for structuring SPs are plainly stated in each product's offering memorandum. These fees typically appear as either a fixed annual fee for the term of the product or as a floating rate fee that is tied to a specified index. Both types of rates are established by reference to historical rates for the specific index and an analysis of the forward interest rate curves based on the term of the product.

Guarantors have a multitude of ways in which they can guarantee Hedge Fund Assets to create SPs. Some guarantors will wrap a guarantee around a fund of hedge funds that makes direct investments in selected hedge funds. The price of the guarantee varies according to the underlying Hedge Fund Asset's allocation, its liquidity and the collective reputation of the underlying managers. Other Providers have their own proprietary Hedge Fund Assets (such as a fund of hedge funds or index) that they manage internally and for which their institution provides a guarantee. In effect, these managers look for distribution channels that can place their products. By far, the most complex and comprehensive undertaking is to set up a platform of Managed Accounts, with a diverse group of managers across the majority of the strategies, from which SPs can be created. Only a few institutions have made the financial and intellectual commitment to this SP platform and further enhanced it with robust risk management tools.

5.5.5 Tax treatment

It is important to analyse the tax ramifications to an investor constituency prior to designing, creating or investing in SPs. This analysis can identify the most efficient product by taking advantage of the flexibility available in structuring these products. Prior to investing in an established structure, investors should examine its tax treatment to assure themselves that they do not experience any unforeseen negative tax consequences. Due to the varied tax treatment based on each individual jurisdiction, developing a general framework for taxation of these products is not meaningful here.

5.6   LOOKING AHEAD

The future of SPs is positive as these products address the needs of investors who want the benefits of hedge funds, but cannot get them efficiently from existing choices. While investors in Europe and Asia have enjoyed the benefits from SPs over the last 5 to 10 years, these products have not been as well received in the United States. We suspect that one of the main reasons is that the benefits of SPs have not been fully understood by investors and/or their advisors. As the benefits become better understood through effective communication, investors will find an advantage in allocating a portion of their portfolios to SPs. Education on the value of these products is a key element in making them attractive to both advisors and investors. Distributors of SPs will need to have a solid education programme in place that can be delivered in a manner that is easy to understand and successfully communicated to potential investors and their advisors.

   With poor stock market performance, we anticipate more demand for SPs, particularly those that offer meaningful transparency, effective risk management, a high degree of liquidity and principal protection. This demand will come from institutional investors such as small to mid-sized pension plans, endowments and foundations that have been frustrated by traditional investment underperformance. These institutional investors are seeking to achieve their investment goals not only by diversifying their portfolios, but also by employing an absolute return approach. In addition, HNW investors will embrace these products as a way of achieving their now-modified retirement goals.

   SPs have not been attractive investments for larger institutional investors because they have the sophistication and critical mass to build a product to their own specifications without the additional cost structures imposed by the SP Provider and the investment advisor on the Hedge Fund Asset. Owing to the fiduciary nature of these institutions, they retain investment consultants that specialize in specific asset classes as a way to augment their own internal expertise. Large institutions are able to overcome transparency issues by virtue of regulatory oversight and by the open communication with individual hedge fund managers that results from their meaningful allocations to the managers.

As the hedge fund industry matures, some managers will restructure their businesses and institutionalize them in an effort to attract new assets. As a result, we believe that the hedge fund industry will become segmented to an extent based on a manager's "institutional" quality. Owing to increased participation by institutional investors who have stringent fiduciary responsibilities, more careful scrutiny of manager's operations and portfolios will become necessary. Managers with well-earned star reputations and limited capacity will continue to attract investors in spite of the limited transparency they provide, longer lockup periods and infrequent liquidity. Others will institutionalize their businesses by building a team concept that can survive the initial founders and diversify their client base–these managers will accept more stringent institutional due diligence and the Managed Account philosophy. Managers on Managed Account platforms will be perceived as meeting strict quality standards because these accounts, which manager's run pari-pasu with their flagship funds, are subject to public scrutiny, stringent risk management and rigorous portfolio analysis techniques.

While some managers may not find the Managed Account platform appealing because they do not want to make their portfolio holdings available to the public, they will still want to give investors some assurance that they comply with their stated investment mandate. Institutional investors will also want to ensure that managers stay within their investment guidelines. As more emphasis is placed on risk management, investors will increasingly demand independent risk management services offered by reputable independent firms that subject a manager's portfolio to extensive risk management analysis and provide assurance to investors that managers are staying within the guidelines of their investment program. Managers may also see the value of this independent oversight as it gives them more credibility with prospects and investors and alleviates some of the "manager event risk" that accompanies an investment made directly in a hedge fund. One of the main reasons this concept has only been implemented on a limited basis is that participants in the industry (managers and investors) have not yet solved the problem of who absorbs the costs for this added level of assurance. A solution to this problem will emerge as the industry continues to mature and institutional investors seek higher levels of comfort.

One advantage for managers to attracting assets via SPs is that these investors are unlikely to invest directly in hedge funds, thus enabling managers to attract funds otherwise not previously available to them. Another advantage of SPs is that managers accepting assets related to SPs are diversifying both their investor base and distribution channels. Finally, most SP buyers have relatively long time horizons, which can result in a more stable asset base for hedge fund managers. These reasons, coupled with the continued "institutionalization" of hedge funds, are making hedge fund managers increasingly receptive to SPs as an attractive source of stable capital for their hedge funds.

Chapter 6

Careers in hedge funds

KATHLEEN A. GRAHAM

6.1 OVERVIEW

Too often when people think of careers in hedge funds, their image is only that of the trader, a person whose mind in a nanosecond moves through world markets noting anomalies, devising and then executing strategies to capture the inherent profit present in these deviations from market efficiencies, all the while waylaying the risk. These traders, however, do not operate in a vacuum – their success and the success of their firms is dependent upon numerous other positions that offer careers in hedge funds equally important to the bottom line.

This chapter will explore all those careers in hedge funds, noting educational and previous work experience requirements, necessary skills and personality aptitudes, the types of funds where these careers most frequently occur, and ending with a prediction of likely growth in each of those areas.

Most hedge funds – like any other financial institution – can be divided into three main employment areas:

A. *BACK OFFICE*: those occupations that sustain the profit-generating activities of the firm but are not directly involved in the actual performance of those actions. The careers in hedge funds that exist in this category are:
   1. **accounting**: *accountants*, *Chief Financial Officers*, and *compliance* personnel
   2. **customer service**: *client* OR *investor relations* staff
   3. **human resources**: *benefits*, *department heads*, and *recruiters* workforce
   4. **legal**: *compliance*, and *General Counsel* employees
   5. **systems/information technology (IT)**: *Chief Information Officer (CIO)*, *developers*, *network*, *database and systems administrators*, *programmers*, *project managers*, and *systems analysts* personnel.
B. *MIDDLE OFFICE*: those positions that ensure that the trades undertaken are correctly noted and their associated risks managed. In a hedge fund, these middle office careers are:

6. **operations**: *Chief Operations Officer (COO), Operations Manager*; and *Operations Specialists* workforce
7. **research** staff: *Analyst, Head of Research*, and *Portfolio Manager*
8. **risk management** employees.

C. *FRONT OFFICE*: the personnel directly responsible for generating the firm's profits and losses. The professions in a hedge fund that are in this category are:

9. **marketing** workforce
10. **quantitative modelers** staff
11. **traders:** *all types of strategies* and *Chief Executive Officer* (CEO) personnel.

Areas that this chapter will not be covering are the current inclusions of private equity investments into hedge fund portfolios and compensation. Because of the recent huge inflow of funds into hedge funds and the relatively few perceived opportunities this current market offers to capture the size returns hedge funds have historically offered their investors, some hedge funds are moving a portion of their resources into private equity investments, which are highly illiquid and of a longer holding period (average is 3 – 5 years before investment is either sold or taken public) than the rest of a hedge fund's profit-raising activities. The careers in this area are similar to the careers found in the private equity field and, because this chapter is about careers in hedge funds – not private equity – this type of hedge fund function will not be reviewed.

As for compensation, alas, there is no statistically significant source of information to draw upon because most of the compensation studies to date have had too few individuals interviewed to make their findings reliable given the following variables:

(1) there are over 10 different strategies (see accompanying chart on page 110 for specifics) that hedge funds can employ with different risk/return payoffs, which means that the compensation will or could be different for each of those strategies.

(2) the size of hedge fund assets under management ranges from under $10 million to over $20 billion, which, in addition to the number employed, also affects how much employees can be paid in general.

(3) hedge funds are located all over the world in both urban and more rural settings with each of these locations facing different tax, healthcare, retirement, education, hire/fire policies and cost of living structures, which all impact compensation dynamics.

If a study does not consider these variables or has too few data points for each of these scenarios, the compensation information can be adversely impacted.

There are firms that do provide comprehensive compensation studies but their results face a different dilemma. To cover the costs of collecting such information, these firms charge a fee that not all hedge funds choose to pay. If a firm opts out of the fee, their information is not included in the study. If a significant number of the different types of hedge funds are not included in these firms' studies, their results are biased in that they are only truly reflective of a subsector of the general hedge fund population, i.e. that sector of firms willing to pay for the compensation study.

To wrap up this discussion about hedge fund careers, one interesting subsector of the hedge fund employment population will be the focus: women. Only a small percentage of all hedge fund professionals are women, says Kristin Fox, Senior Vice President of News and Research for *Lipper HedgeWorld* and a board member of the organization, 100 Women in Hedge Funds. This chapter, therefore, ends with some interesting observations about the special issues these women face when they choose a career in hedge funds.

The arrangement of this reading material is so that it can be read from start to finish or by just going directly to the chapter topics that are of interest. More information can also be found by searching these topics titles on line or by subscribing to the free e-mail newsletter, *HQ's Financial Views*, to be found at www.hqsearch.com.

6.2 BACK OFFICE CAREERS

6.2.1 Accounting

Types of accounting positions and typical duties

Accountant: Manage the monthly accounting process and oversee the fund administrator's net asset value (NAV) computation. Review fund holdings for new trades and changes in fund positions. Maintain a schedule of investments as accounting support. Prepare mid-month and month-end performance estimates. Review management fee and incentive fee calculations. Coordinate annual audit. Review financial statements. Assist with the accounting structure for new deals. Perform due diligence on underlying hedge fund-audited financials. Assist/support CFO with special projects. In some hedge funds some or all of the accounting functions are outsourced to dedicated accounting/operations speciality firms.

Chief financial officer (CFO): Prepare and analyze budgets, monthly financial reporting and forecasts. Participate in preparation of high level analysis and presentations to senior management and Board. Lead discussions with heads of departments and provide value-added recommendations to meet budgetary targets. Manage the financial affairs of the company; producing management accounts, financial statements; communicating with shareholders at the company level and at the fund level coordinating with custodians, legal advisors and administrators; verifying NAVs; communicating with investors; setting up infrastructure of funds; and maintaining direct contact with underlying hedge funds managers. In larger hedge funds, supervise staff to ensure accurate and timely completion of all of the above responsibilities. In smaller hedge funds the CFO might also be the account-ant, compliance, and the COO all rolled into one with minimal or no staff.

Compliance: Provide high-quality advice and assistance in relation to new busi-ness initiatives to ensure a robust compliance infrastructure is implemented for any new initiatives. Review due diligence, implementing suitability checks on prospec-tive clients and providing advice to business areas on regulatory issues. Develop and implement procedures to ensure compliance with legal and regulatory require-ments. In smaller hedge funds or for those with only proprietary funds or few in numbers of investors, the compliance role does not even legally need to exist in some countries.

Educational requirements

A US Bachelors degree (or its overseas equivalent) is the minimal educational background for *hedge fund accountants*. Most funds prefer the undergraduate degree's major to be in Accounting or Finance. If the GPAs are not 3.5/4.0 (or equivalent percentage for schools with different scale ranges) or higher, a plausi-ble explanation for the ranking will be necessary to even be considered. Class grades in core accounting classes must all be "A's" or "B's".

A US Certified Public Accountant (CPA) (or its overseas equivalent) is always preferred (and many times is required) as an additional accreditation. A common question asked is if an individual passed their CPA exam on the first sitting as this achievement is another favorable mark for hiring in this field, although some who did not pass all levels the first time through do get hired by hedge funds of all assets under management (AUM) sizes.

As individuals in the different accounting functions move up the career levels to the highest accounting function, the *Chief Financial Officer* (*CFO*) level, a Masters in Taxation, Computer Systems, Finance, Accounting, or a general MBA is also becoming more of a requirement instead of the optional "plus" that it used to be. The larger the AUM the hedge fund has, the more the university has to be a top tier name, especially at the Masters level and frequently also for the undergraduate degree.

Compliance positions come in two flavors: ones that appear in this section that require a strong accounting background (CPA a must, Masters a plus) to focus more on the financial statements and financial reporting compliance issues and the other type that requires a J.D. legal degree to concentrate more on the legal regu-latory topics.

Work experience

Accounting staff at all levels are rarely hired without previous experience in hedge fund accounting. The audit, tax and general accounting hedge fund practices in the financial services groups of consulting firms, therefore, are the major training grounds for future hedge fund accountants and CFOs. Given the demanding hours and the wide variety of hedge funds these individuals are exposed to, it is no wonder that hedge funds regularly recruit their accounting staff at all levels from this pool. Another source of experienced accountants are the smaller AUM hedge funds where the individuals, because of the size of the firm, get to work with a much larger breadth of responsibility than their counterparts in larger funds.

Hedge funds usually hire their *compliance* staff either from other hedge funds or from the audit or legal department personnel working for an exchange or a government financial services regulatory body.

Skills and personality aptitudes

- Great attention to detail and process.
- Committed to performing work perfectly.
- Non-combative personality that, on the other hand, is not easily convinced to change opinions/facts when aggressively confronted by others impacted by their findings.
- A smart probing mind that seeks to identify and understand what the underlying factors that are creating the observed facts.
- Computer and technology savvy.
- Good communication skills.
- A professional that commands respect.

Growth prognosis: *Fantastic!*

Because of all the increased regulation confronting all types of companies – including hedge funds – worldwide, accounting and compliance are two of the hottest industry sectors. Demand definitely outstrips supply currently and until these dynamics change, which does not appear likely for the near future, increasing compensation levels and a large choice of positions await just about everyone in this field who can crunch the numbers, grasp the concepts, and master the technology.

6.2.2   Customer service

Types of customer service positions and typical duties

Client or investor relations: Whether called Client Relations or Investor Relations, is responsible overall for: all investor communications including investor queries and investor updates; liaison with marketing; meetings and conference calls with key stakeholders; customized reporting for clients and the preparation of hedge fund and general market summaries and investor letters. Writes newsletters, which includes gathering market data and meeting with internal managers to format content. Identify speaking engagement possibilities at relevant conferences. Prepare and dispatch requests for proposals, or as they are known in the industry, RFPs.

Larger AUMs hedge funds may have a designated investor relations person who is solely responsible for fielding calls from investors with other individuals assuming the other functions given above.

Educational requirements

Minimally a US Bachelor's degree (or overseas equivalent) is required although additional accreditations are a plus. Liberal arts degrees in general or with Marketing, English, or Communication major work just as well as a finance degree for client relations position.

Work experience

Many hedge funds hire this type of employee from traditional money management or corporate investor relations departments, hedge fund publications, or from other hedge funds.

Skills and personality aptitudes

- Outstanding writing and publicity layout experience.
- Polished professional demeanor.
- Ability to interact with the media and high net worth individuals in a positive manner.
- Knowledge about the basics of finance, markets, and products.

Growth prognosis: Fair

With marketing constraints on hedge funds tight and funds flowing in at volume records, there is minimal interest by management in expanding investor relations because at this point in the life cycle of hedge funds, there is a limited need to grow these services.

6.2.3   Human resources (HR)

Types of human resources positions and typical duties

Benefits: In countries where national healthcare is not provided, responsible for identifying and implementing good health plans at minimal cost. Oversee ongoing paperwork administration and answer employee benefits questions. Explain retirement plans to employees. The benefits area is one that is open to being outsourced partially or completely to a dedicated benefits administration firm.

Department heads: Execute a wide range of responsibilities, including answering employee questions, helping coworkers work out disagreements, and making sure that supervisors treat employees fairly. Help maintain working relationships between employers and employees. Oversee hiring, benefits, salaries, training, and more. Set up employee evaluation programs thorough knowledge of state and federal employment and labor laws and personnel practices.

In the smallest hedge funds, the head of the firm might also be the person in charge of all HR functions. As the size of the hedge fund grows, usually the human resources duties are transferred first to one dedicated HR person in charge of all benefits and recruitment followed by even more HR staff additions dedicated to specific areas. The training and development function is another area that is open to being outsourced partially or completely to a dedicated training and development firm.

Recruiters: Responsible for implementing recruitment and selection strategies throughout the full recruitment process cycle from development of initial contact database through sourcing candidates, screening, interviewing, compensation research, analyzing background checks, checking references and negotiating offers to ensure that the staffing needs of the organization are met. Thorough knowledge of state and federal employment and labor laws and personnel practices is required. Some hedge funds HR departments choose to outsource their overflow or difficult job searches to professional retained or contingency search firms.

Educational requirements

A US Bachelors degree (or overseas equivalent); liberal arts degrees in general or with Business, Marketing, English, or Communication major works just as well as an Organizational Development concentration for lower level HR positions. At the HR Director and head of HR department level, a Master of Business Administration in Business Policy (Strategy) or Organizational Behavior is a powerful plus to add to a resume.

Work experience

Experience in human resources, preferably from a financial services firm or from a retained financial services executive search firm, is required with demonstrated experience and technical knowledge in some or all of the areas of responsibility. Previous HR work experience with a hedge fund is also always desirable.

Skills and personality aptitudes

- Articulate with excellent communication skills and a flexible interpersonal style.
- Strong initiative and follow-through, self-motivated and highly organized.
- Able to build effective relationships with colleagues and employees at varying levels within the firm.
- Multi-tasker who enjoys working with people.
- Resourceful and creative approach to candidate research and development if involved with recruitment.

Growth prognosis: Fair.
As a staff area, human resources is run "lean and mean" so there will not be more positions in this area than absolutely needed.

6.2.4   Legal

Types of legal positions and typical duties
Compliance: Provide high-quality advice and assistance in relation to new business initiatives to ensure a robust compliance infrastructure is implemented for any new initiatives. Review due diligence, implementing suitability checks on prospective clients and providing advice to business areas on regulatory issues. Develop and implement procedures to ensure compliance with legal and regulatory requirements. In charge of all regulations for the fund, including policies and procedures, code of ethics, portfolio management, and investigations.
General counsel: Undertake various kinds of legal tasks ranging from reading complex legal documents and advising on prospects of litigation in various countries to interacting with boards of directors.

Educational requirements
US J.D. (or its overseas equivalent) and a US Bachelor's degree (or its overseas equivalent) are both required.

Work experience
A large percentage of General Counsels and Compliance personnel start their careers working with hedge funds as part of a law firm's staff before migrating over to work in-house for just one fund. Others were previously working for a regulatory or government agency that interacts with some segment of the hedge fund or money management industry.

As stated earlier, *compliance* positions come in two flavors: those requiring a strong accounting background (CPA a must, Masters a plus) to focus more on the financial statements and financial reporting compliance issues and the other type described in this section that requires a J.D. legal degree to concentrate more on the legal regulatory topics.

Skills and personality aptitudes
- Excellent legal skills.
- Grasp of obtuse concepts quickly with an ability to communicate that information in easy to understand presentations.
- Attention to both detail and the "big picture".
- Succinct.
- A forward-looking approach to avoid litigious situations.

Growth prognosis: Fair

Just like human resources, legal is a staff area. Therefore, it, too, is run "lean and mean" so there will not be more positions in this area than absolutely needed.

6.2.5   Systems/information technology (IT)

Types of systems/IT positions and typical duties

The range of positions in the computer technology area that supports a hedge fund's activities is phenomenally diverse. For example, in the smallest shops all that might be present are some desktop computers (state of the art, of course) with Bloomberg access. Yet the largest hedge funds, in the computer software area alone, can have application developers, client/server developers, database administrators, database developers, data warehouse developers, information system architects, programmers, project managers, software support engineers, and system analysts – just to name a few. Then more individuals are probably working on the computer hardware side to ensure compatibility and cost/benefit analysis of any equipment purchased. Others are likely to specialize in security to keep hackers out. Some more focus on how to farm the internet globally to identify and process in real time all the various seemingly unrelated pieces of information that when added together might provide some very valuable trading information. Heading up all these efforts is a Chief Information Officer, who is also known as a Chief Technology Officer. So as you read this section's descriptions, know that there's many more IT career choice possibilities inherent within a hedge fund structure than what is covered here.

Chief information or technology officer (*CIO or CTO*): Lead the delivery and support of all IT infrastructure services.

Developers: Develop software that works closely with a database by creating the computer programs that will make possible whatever objectives were proposed at inception by the systems analyst. If lead developer, who is also called a *system architect*, put together the framework of the software project, choosing to focus on the most important features that need to be present within the software to optimize its success.[1]

Network, database and systems administrators: Make sure that the network, database or system is available to all the intended users and programs at all times.[2]

Programmers: Write the code that will make the software perform according to the developer's instructions.

---

[1]http://www.mariosalexandrou.com/glossary
[2]http://www.mariosalexandrou.com/glossary

Project managers: Plan, organize, and direct the process and resources of the software project that the developer has created through to successful completion.

Systems analysts: Research, plan and recommend software and systems choices to meet hedge fund's technology needs. Develop cost analyses, design considerations, implementation timelines, and general feasibility studies of proposed computer systems before making recommendations to senior management.[3]

Educational requirements

A US Bachelors degree (or its overseas equivalent) in Computer Science, Software Engineering, Management Information Systems, Mathematics, Finance, etc... is the minimally acceptable academic credentials. Hint: there's no such thing as knowing too many languages, systems, etc. in an IT career so continuous learning of the latest developments is almost always required.

Work experience requirements

For each IT career described, specific product, process, and computer languages are necessary to even be considered as a candidate for that position. Must possess extensive business knowledge across key financial instruments. Prior relevant work experience need not always be with a hedge fund but is preferred that it at least be with another financial services firm.

Skills and personality aptitudes

- Logical mind combined with good communication skills.
- Ability to understand business and trading practices, conceptualize complex product ideas, and figure out new ways to overcome challenges.

Growth prognosis: Good

Despite the outsourcing of many IT functions to India, which has caused a glut of qualified IT job candidates domestically, having the fastest most comprehensive computer systems to capture and deliver the real-time information to front office so they can react quickly enough to gain the profit from market inefficiencies is absolutely critical. Given the consequences of delivery failure, most hedge funds prefer to keep these functions in house and state of the art. Hence, the hiring, rewarding, and promoting of the smartest and best IT personnel is a trend that should continue to grow.

---

[3]www.course.com/careers/glossary/itjobs.cfm

6.3   MIDDLE OFFICE CAREERS

6.3.1   Operations

Types of operations positions and typical duties

Chief operations officer (COO): Oversee operations team and get involved in structuring new funds from an operational perspective. With hedge funds having smaller AUMs, the COO role may be combined with the CFO role or be the person actually performing all of the operational work.

Operations manager: Responsible for performance reporting, new accounts, fund operations, and data integrity across all funds. Help in settling trades, managing cash flow and monitoring risk. Involved with and reviews all breaks and settlements of positions. Work with CFO and COO.

Operations specialists: Work with traders, counterparties and operations team-mates to process confirms, trade settlements, non-dollar funding, and trade reconciliation.

Educational requirements

US Bachelors degree (or overseas equivalent) a must.

Work experience requirements

Does not need to have worked previously in a hedge fund (although having that type of background is a great plus); just needs a proven track record managing internal and external relationships in a complex financial services industry. Needs broad product knowledge covering the specific products their hedge fund trades in plus up to date knowledge of how the systems the firms they interact with when balancing trades, etc. work. Should have exposure to trading P&L plus dealt with prime brokers and custodians. Must have prime brokerage reconciliations experience and at management level experience with managing trading assistants.

Skills and personality aptitudes

- Excellent communications and computer skills.
- Reliable and highly organized with strong commitment to keeping processes working on time and perfectly.
- Team player.

Growth prognosis: Slow

One of the areas hedge funds are able to outsource is the operations area. Couple this fact with technology still gaining the flexibility to replace people in the workforce plus the high cost of hiring because of regulatory and/or healthcare costs and you will understand why growth in this field is predicted to be slow.

6.3.2   Research

Types of research positions and typical duties

The research positions in hedge funds are quite similar to the positions in traditional money management firms in role and title. The role of research personnel is to analyze the performance of asset(s), how those asset(s) react and to what variables from historical and/or current perspectives, then use that information to suggest what the probable future course and related value of that asset is likely to be. If the research personnel are quantitatively inclined, statistics are likely to be employed to determine the probabilities of each possible future position occurring. Although the overall functions might be similar except from a seniority or depth perspective, the titles usually are: *Analysts*, *Head of Research*, and *Portfolio Manager* with a description of their asset or geographic coverage area usually right in front of or contained within their title, i.e. Equity Risk Arbitrage Analyst.

In smaller AUM hedge funds, the research positions might not be present as a separate multi-person department but rather exist as one of many functions carried on by the principals or by a person who supports them in multiple roles. Of course, as the research function is assumed by individuals wearing other hats, many times the research function is then considered part of the front office.

Educational requirements

US Bachelors degree (or overseas equivalent) in Finance, Math, Statistics, or similar fields are required for Analysts level positions. However, higher levels prefer a PhD in those same concentrations. Grades and reputation of education institutions attended are important to those hiring individuals for these types of positions, with the emphasis on higher required ratings increasing the larger the AUM the fund has.

Work experience requirements

A successful track record and experience working for a money management firm with the capability of making the mental shift to a more short-term hold strategy is acceptable. Of course, individuals with similar backgrounds already working for another hedge fund are always of interest.

Skills and personality aptitudes

- Analytical nature capable of sorting through a myriad of facts to correctly identify the most likely probable real-world outcomes.
- Relishes achieving on an absolute returns basis.

Growth prognosis: Good

A fundamental or technical analysis of any asset of interest provides value to many hedge funds so hiring is likely to continue in this area.

6.3.3   Risk management

Types of risk management positions and typical duties

Analyze exposure to risk on a trade by trade basis and also on an overall portfolio basis, determine how to mitigate the risk present, make recommendations to senior management based upon those determinations, and then execute approved action. Ensure continual monitoring of key risks remains in place and is constantly improved upon.

Once again, the function of a risk manager as a stand-alone entity or department increases as the size of AUM increases. Therefore, at smaller hedge funds this function is probably relegated to being a responsibility of one of the more analytical senior personnel.

Educational requirements

A US Bachelors degree (or its overseas equivalent) is the minimal educational background for *risk manager*s. Most funds prefer the undergraduate degree's major to be in Accounting or Finance. If the GPAs are not 3.5/4.0 (or equivalent percentage for schools with different scale ranges) or higher, a plausible explanation for the ranking will be necessary to even be considered. Class grades in core classes must all be "A's" or "B's".

A Master's or a PhD is almost always a requirement. In fact, the larger the AUM the hedge fund has, the more the university has to be a top tier name, especially at the Masters level and frequently also for the undergraduate degree.

Work experience requirements

Experience as a risk manager at most financial institutions with knowledge of the specific trading strategy and assets is the preferred background.

In smaller AUM hedge funds, the risk management positions might not be present as a separate multi-person department but rather exist as one of many functions carried on by the principals or by a person who supports them in multiple roles. Of course, as the risk management function is assumed by individuals wearing other hats, many times the risk management function is then considered part of the front office.

Skills and personality aptitudes

- Excellent attention to detail and numerical abilities.
- Strong computer and technology skills.

- Articulate team player.
- Forward looking thinking process capable of ferreting out potential risks and then creatively solving them.

Growth prognosis: Great

With only accounting and compliance positions more in demand, risk management is experiencing a strong interest by hedge funds (and, quite frankly, all corporations and financial institutions) as a means to manage uncertainty and dissipate risk in a world right now that's hard to predict what sentiment will be from day to day.

6.4   FRONT OFFICE CAREERS

6.4.1   Marketing

Types of marketing positions and typical duties

Marketing in a hedge fund is usually sales – not market research. There are two types that marketing staff sells to:

- Broker/dealers: more of a "sales-like" relationship development promoted by many hedge funds management, there may even be dedicated individuals to this function in larger AUM hedge funds because enhancing the relationship with one's prime broker (the one broker that a hedge fund runs all of its trading through to avoid signaling its intentions to the market) may have profitable overtones as the prime broker also may supply custodial, clearing and research services,[4] potential employee referrals, trade ideas, etc…
- Investors – both institutional and/or high net worth – to encourage them to devote some of their funds to their particular hedge fund institution. Usually who they are selling to is departmentalized into specific geographic or profile characteristics, i.e. new business development to Japanese institutional investors.

Educational requirements

US Bachelor's degree (or overseas equivalent) is all that is required. Liberal arts degrees in general or with Marketing, Psychology, or Communication major work just as well as a finance degree for marketing positions.

Work experience requirements

For more senior positions, a rolodex of already established relationships and a track record of past sales success is a must. For more junior positions, a history of successful sales of some type of intangible financial services product will do.

---

[4]www.advisor.ca/product/canHedge/article.jsp, definition of a prime broker.

Skills and personality aptitudes

- A persona that is likeable yet professional.
- Good follow through in taking care of the large number of minutia that cements a successful sale and ensures good referrals elsewhere.
- Ability to "close the deal" – i.e. bring the relationship to where it actually manifests in a profit for the hedge fund.

Growth prognosis: Great

Although funds are flowing in freely without much assistance, marketing plays a profit-generating role…and roles that increase profits are usually on the "must grow" list. In fact, for smaller AUM hedge funds, the role of the marketer in increasing their asset size is critical.

6.4.2   Quantitative modelers

Types of quantitative modelers' positions and typical duties

Design and implement sophisticated derivatives pricing models – also known as financial engineers, quantitative modelers design and implement sophisticated derivatives pricing models so that traders can have a platform by which to judge whether an asset is over or under priced.

Educational requirements

Bachelors (or overseas equivalent) with advanced degrees (PhD is a plus, Masters is a must) in mathematics, physics or related field required.

Work experience requirements

Quantitative modeling is the one area where true "rocket scientists", i.e. someone working on an advanced educational or government scientific endeavor with no previous hedge fund or financial services experience can start with a hedge fund.

Skills and personality aptitudes

- Brilliant and adept at working with extremely complex mathematical equations to arrive at correct real world answers.
- Good communication skills.
- Fast-forward thinking mind.

Growth prognosis: Great

With hedge funds scrambling to find ways to reach for the returns their investors are convinced they're capable of delivering, accurate reliable quantitative modeling that delivers real world asset prices is a core necessity.

6.4.3 Traders

Types of trading positions and typical duties

Chief executive officer (CEO): generally the top performing trader who eventually becomes the owner or the person in charge of either the firm he started with at a lower position or at a firm he starts.

Trader: Anyone who as a profession buys and sells assets on a regular basis in order to make a profit. Hedge fund traders tend to specialize in any of the following strategies:

- *convertible bond arbitrage*: the in synch purchase of a bond with an option to exchange it for a fixed number of stock shares and a "borrowed" sale of same firm's common stock to attain profit through price differences while protecting initial investment.
- *emerging markets*: the buying of stocks and/or bonds in less economically developed countries that are showing strengthening economies in order to acquire potential profits embedded in their exponential start-up growth phases.
- *equity market neutral*: the buying of stock and/or selling of "borrowed" stock to maintain a portfolio net exposure of zero dollars, zero beta, or zero sector orientation so that there exists no inherent market directional bets occurring in order to gain steady returns with minimal risk.
- *event-driven risk [merger] arbitrage*: the buying of stock and/or selling of "borrowed" stock OR an in synch stock purchase with a sale of "borrowed" stock and/or convertible bond of a firm expected to merge or be acquired by another company in order to capture price movements from this consequential corporate event.
- *event-driven distressed/high yield arbitrage*: the buying of stock and/or selling of "borrowed" stock OR an in synch stock purchase with a sale of "borrowed" stock and/or convertible bond of a firm expected to become financially distressed or bankrupt in order to capture price movements from this consequential corporate event.
- *event-driven regulation D*: the buying of stock and/or selling of "borrowed" stock OR an in synch stock purchase with a sale of "borrowed" stock and/or convertible bond of a micro or small capitalized public firm expected to raise private monies in order to capture price movements from this consequential corporate event.
- *fixed income arbitrage*: the buying of interest rate securities and the selling of the "borrowed" related interest rate securities on a global basis to net price incongruities that offer steady returns with low volatility.
- *global macro*: the buying of any (including derivatives) asset and the selling of the "borrowed" same asset on a global basis based on an opinion of overall market direction in reaction to economic events in order to attain profit from price directional changes.

- *long/short equity*: the buying of stock while selling the "borrowed" stock with maybe some balancing futures/options to bet on an interesting sector's direction to gain profit from price directional changes.
- *managed futures*: (a) the buying or selling of a financial, commodity, and/or currency futures contract on the margin to place a directional stake on an opinion regarding future prices in order to secure a profit from the price directional change; (b) the buying of a financial, commodity, and/or currency futures contract on the margin while selling on the margin a related financial, commodity, and/or currency future contract to capture profit when a market event occurs.
- *short sellers*: the buying of less stock and/or derivative instrument than the selling of the same "borrowed" stock and/or derivative instrument with the aim of buying them back at a lower price to acquire the profit from market inefficiencies that create pricing inaccuracies.[5]

If the hedge fund a trader works for employs traders using only one of the above methods, then the hedge fund is called a *single strategy* hedge fund. Conversely, if the hedge fund employs a number of traders using different strategies, then the hedge fund is referred to as a *multi-strategy* hedge fund. A special sub sector of multi-strategy hedge funds is the *fund of funds* hedge fund; i.e. a hedge fund that invests in other hedge funds.

Another special sub sector of hedge funds is the *proprietary trading firm*, which is a hedge fund that accepts no outside investors' monies – the firm's principals trade with only their own funds. Because there is no accountability to others that would require staying true to one type of investment strategy, these firms often mix the above strategies because their only goal is to optimize their profits and they can afford to be more opportunistic with their choices of employed strategies.

Educational requirements

Back in the wild and wooly beginning days of hedge funds when a certain breed of traders existed called "cowboys" because they took bets based mostly on intuitive hunches (versus the "quants" who researched out their strategies), a US Bachelors degree (or its overseas equivalent) was all that was required to become a trader. Nowadays even the least quantitative strategies, like the long/short equities shops, usually require a Masters degree in Analytic Finance, Financial Mathematics, or similar academic credentials.

There are a number of reasons for the increase in educational requirements, some of which may be:

---

[5]*Financial Engineering News*, November/December 2003, "Alternative Investments A to Z", p5, Kathy Graham

- An advanced degree in a particular area ensures that all individuals in a very fast paced rapidly changing environment where miscommunications can be disastrous share a common language.
- An advanced degree serves as a barrier to entry so that the multitudes who would like to work for a hedge fund have a significant hurdle to jump before being qualified to do so.
- An advanced degree ensures that all traders understand the complex fundamentals of the industry; i.e. how markets operate; options, assets, and derivatives pricing theories and tools; behavioral elements, etc. . . .

In addition to having an advanced degree, the overall GPA and the ranking of the university attended is very important to some hedge funds, with higher grades and higher ranking being considered the profile that best fits their firms.

Work experience requirements
Two years at a bulge bracket (i.e. top tier) investment bank in their derivatives, corporate finance, high yield or other departments where intricate financing in a fast paced market-dependent environment with long hours as the norm is considered a great training ground for junior traders.

For more experienced individuals, an excellent desk trading track record is the key. Occasionally, someone from the traditional money management market makes a successful transition to the alternatives side. Such a transition may be difficult, however, as the traditional money management's standard is to measure success in relationship to a benchmark (i.e. outperformed the S&P 500 by 30 basis points) and is a long-term buy/hold strategy for the most part whereas the hedge fund trader's standard is to measure success in absolute returns (i.e. earned 50% return on money invested with a specific trader or strategy) and is a short term "buy and sell for immediate optimal profit" strategy so the timing of moving positions can be different.

Skills and personality aptitudes

- Brilliant.
- Has a "map" in his head that enables him to see the directional movements of all of the information pieces to the point the likely outcome of their interaction stands out clearly.
- Succinct.
- Focused.
- Driven to succeed.
- Outstanding computer and technology skills.
- Tolerance for ever present risk and uncertainty.

Growth prognosis: Good

An outstanding trader provides value to his firm, himself, and the market in general because it's the smart traders who capture the inefficiencies, thus forcing asset prices to their true values.

6.5   SPECIAL ISSUES THAT WOMEN FACE

In this author's opinion, there is only one special issue that women in hedge funds face that they do not face in all the other financial services professions (beyond the financial service sector of banks, investment banks, real estate firms, private equity/venture capital, money management, research, and consulting, the author does not have enough experience to comment on). That issue is that there are not enough women with advanced quantitative degrees, which means that because the majority of hedge funds are in strategies requiring such degrees there are not enough women hedge fund traders, quantitative modelers, risk managers, or researchers.

What is causing this phenomenon is perplexing. Approximately 20 – 25% of all MBA students at the top tier universities are women, who obviously are smart enough to study the quantitative financial topics because they were admitted to these schools. There are no barriers to entry once in one of these universities that prevent women from taking these courses. In fact, the author can personally attest that the professors and males students at all of her analytical finance, econometrics and statistics classes at The University of Chicago were always extremely helpful and nice. Yet whenever the author took one of the "quant" classes, there were few other women in these classes as compared to the number of women attending the other types of MBA classes. Unfortunately, these numbers of women in advanced quantitative courses are not atypical despite the best ongoing efforts of many leading universities to change this trend. Until this trend is reversed, the number of women even qualified for some of the highest paying positions in hedge funds will be small.

Outside of this puzzling self-discriminating factor, women in hedge funds face the same issues that women in professional positions everywhere face: lack of child and family support systems, harassment, lower pay, exclusion from informal and/or formal networks, etc. . . . Rather than dwell on the too well-known negatives, this concluding section chooses to focus on what senior professional women in many great organizations have found to work in overcoming or at least minimizing the obstacles so that they can break through those glass ceilings one way or another. The following is a sampling of that sage advice:

1. Find bosses that are good mentors. People with daughters or granddaughters, career wives or career mothers are an outstanding source. If you can't find a mentor, read up on all the great people in your field and create a composite mentor that you can learn from.

2. Do not count on those who only like you when you are down, will not share, or are stuck in a homogenous reality. The world is full of plenty of other people willing to help you help yourself up…if you are willing in return to give something back.

3. Find something you can do for those who choose to assist you – surely one of your great skills complements a weakness or lack of time that your "mentor for the moment" would value.

4. Remember to reach down and sideways to help the next person up, too. In doing so, you're creating an invaluable support network of people you enjoy working with at all levels.

5. Find a way that is you to make men feel comfortable working with you.

6. Do your best…and then some.

7. Make sure that you inform (note: informing is different than bragging) people about what you do best and your achievements.

8. If you don't ask for it, you'll never get it…so ask for what you want or need.

9. Faced with the uncomfortable, suck it in and walk it off.

10. Read Gail Evans' books, *Play Like a Man Win Like a Woman: What Men Know about Success that Women Need to Learn* and *She Wins You Win: The Most Important Rule Every Businesswoman Needs to Know*. They offer fantastic advice from a former White House aide and CNN's first female Executive Vice President…plus they are easy and enjoyable to read.

11. Find your sustainable competitive advantage, work it, and guard it.

12. Find or create the environment that suits you best because in hedge funds you do not have to be big to make a lot of money – you just have to own a computer, have access to a reliable financial news and data source, and be very good at what you do.

There are over ten different strategies that hedge funds can employ with different risk/return payoffs, which means that the compensation will or could be different for each of those strategies

Common hedge fund strategies, risk/reward profiles

Product	Types	Reward	Risk
Hedge Fund: a private investment conduit organized as a limited partnership where investors' assets are pooled	*Convertible Bond Arbitrage*: in synch purchase a bond with option to exchange it for a fixed number of stock shares & "borrowed" sale of same firm's common stock.	Attain profit through price differences while protecting initial investment.	Lack of underlying product availability; performance measurement shortcomings; transparency issues; liquidity, interest rate, & failure rate risk are the risks inherent in all of these different strategy types.
	Emerging Markets: buying stocks &/or bonds in less economically developed countries with strengthening economies.	Acquire potential profits embedded in exponential start-up growth phase.	
	Equity Market Neutral: buying stock/selling "borrowed" stock to maintain a portfolio net exposure of zero dollars, zero beta, or zero sector = no market direction bets.	Gain steady returns with minimal risk.	
	Event-Driven: buying stock &/or selling "borrowed" stock OR in synch stock purchase with sale of "borrowed" stock &/or convertible bond of firm expected to have one of these events: 1) *Risk (Merger) Arbitrage*: merger or acquisition; 2) *Distressed or High Yield Securities*: financially distressed or bankrupt company; 3) *Regulation D*: micro/small cap public firm raising private monies.	Capture price movements of consequential corporate events.	
	Fixed Income Arbitrage: buy interest rate security/sell "borrowed" related interest rate security on a global basis.	Net price incongruities that offer steady returns with low volatility	
	Global Macro: buy any (including derivative) asset/sell "borrowed" same asset on a global basis based on an opinion of overall market direction in reaction to economic event.	Attain profit from price directional changes.	
	Long/Short Equity: buy stock while selling "borrowed" stock with maybe some balancing futures/options to bet on an interesting sector's direction.	Gain profit from price directional changes.	

Managed Futures:

(a) the buying or selling of a financial, commodity, and/or currency futures contract on the margin to place a directional stake on an opinion regarding future prices in order to secure a profit from the price directional change

(b) the buying of a financial, commodity, and/or currency futures contract on the margin while selling on the margin a related financial, commodity, and/or currency futures contract to capture profit when a market event occurs.

(a) Gain profit from price directional changes.

(b) Capture profit when market event occurs.

Multi-Strategy:

(a) *Single Manager* with a strategy of investing/shifting in/between multiple types of hedge funds but all in one portfolio

(b) *Fund of Funds* a hedge fund that invests in other hedge funds.

Short Sellers: buying less stock &/or derivative than selling same "borrowed" stock &/or derivative with aim of buying them back at a lower price.

Single Manager gains greater choice of investments with lower costs than a fund of funds

while

Funds of Funds offer greater diversification. Both offer more investment oversight.

Acquire profit from market inefficiencies creating pricing inaccuracies.

---

*Operational risks of key person, settlement, judge track record, claim liability, disputed/contingent claims, holding period, liquidation, tax issues, and compliance/IT/legal/infrastructure are similar to other privately-held businesses. *Financial Engineering News*, November/December 2003, "Alternative Investments A to Z", p5, Kathy Graham.

Chapter 7

A liquidity haircut for hedge funds[1]

HARI KRISHNAN[2] AND IZZY NELKEN[3]

7.1 INTRODUCTION

Since the 1950s, mean variance optimization has been widely used to construct port-folios of traditional assets, such as stocks and bonds. Over the past 10 years, alterna-tive investments such as hedge funds have risen in prominence. There are currently more than 6,000 registered hedge funds worldwide. Many have performed well in bull and bear markets and there has been a significant flow of assets into hedge funds.

It is natural to ask the question: how much of an investor's portfolio should be allocated to a specific hedge fund or a portfolio of hedge funds? The usual approach has been to incorporate hedge funds in a mean variance framework. However, many hedge funds have outperformed stocks and bonds (in a risk-adjusted sense) over the past few years; thus, a naïve optimizer would allocate nearly all assets to these funds rather than traditional assets. Many fund of funds have capped the allocation to hedge funds at 20 – 30% in an ad hoc way. This reflects the idea that there are sub-tle risks in hedge fund investing; we list some of these below:

- The 'true' volatility of a hedge fund may be much larger than its historical volatility. Managers who trade illiquid assets tend to receive disproportionately large allocations according to mean variance theory. Since the assets do not trade much, portfolio returns tend to have a large serial correlation from month to month. This lowers the calculated historical volatility.

- Fung and Hseih (1997) have noted that the returns of trend following future managers can be extremely non-normal and use an options pricing approach to model them. Many managers are natural sellers of credit or liquidity premia. This means that they generate attractive Sharpe ratios under normal conditions, while retaining a small probability of a large negative return.

[1]Originally published in Risk Magazine April 2003.
[2]Vice President, Investment Management Division, Morgan Stanley (hari.krishnan@morganstanley.com).
[3]President, Super Computer Consulting (izzy@supercc.com).

- Funds that blow up tend to disappear from the radar screen. Schneeweis and Spurgin (2000) among others, have documented how hedge fund returns can be upwardly skewed by survivorship bias. Many composite measures of hedge fund performance only include funds that have survived up to the present. Thus, these composites tend not to include the funds that closed or did not perform well in the past. Many funds, such as Long Term Capital Management, have had periods of stellar performance before blowing up.

In this chapter, we focus on the liquidity risk that a hedge fund investor faces. An investor faces liquidity risk since capital is typically locked up in a fund for a year or two before it can be taken out.[4] During the lockup period, a manager can vary his strategy, increase his risk exposure or worse, blow up. To our knowledge, a liquidity haircut for hedge funds has not yet been quantified and we make a calculation here. The haircut can be used when making an allocation decision between a hedge fund and a traditional asset or fund. Our method consists of two main steps. First, we extend the chapter of Goetzmann, Ibbotson and Ross (working paper) and study the value of the incentive clause to a hedge fund manager. We qualitatively describe how a hedge fund manager can optimally vary his leverage to maximize his expected profit, using an option pricing approach.

Second, we assume that an investor holds a portfolio consisting of a traditional fund and a hedge fund. While the hedge fund manager wants to maximize the value of his incentive clause, the investor wants to maximize the *return/risk* ratio of his portfolio. Thus, the hedge fund manager and investor are playing a cat and mouse game. If the investor had unrestricted liquidity, he could rebalance between the hedge fund and traditional asset in response to a change in leverage or the probability of a blow up. Since he cannot rebalance, he either needs to discount the return or increase the volatility of the hedge fund before he makes a decision to invest. We adapt a method of Longstaff (forthcoming) to calculate the illiquidity premium.

We conclude the chapter with a numerical example, where we show that the volatility of a hedge fund should be increased by a factor of about 10% over its historical value, to account for illiquidity.

7.2 VALUING THE HEDGE FUND MANAGER'S CONTRACT

Goetzmann, Ingersoll and Ross (working paper) have modelled the evolution of the high water mark and calculated the expected value of the contract to a manager.

---

[4]If a hedge fund has a 1 year lockup, funds can typically only be taken out at the end of the calendar year following the year of investment. Thus, an investor who allocates money in January 2002 can only take the money out in December 2003 and the effective lockup period is 2 years.

Suppose that a fund's asset level is given by $S(t)$ at time t and that $S(t)$ evolves according to a discrete lognormal diffusion with drift $\mu - c - W$ and volatility σ. The asset level drift μ (assumed to be greater than 0) and management fee c are constant. Funds are added or redeemed at the rate $W = W(t,S)$. If an investor redeems, then $W > 0$, else $W \leq 0$. Thus $S(t + \Delta t) = S(t) + (\mu - W - c)S(t)\Delta t + \sigma S(t)\sqrt{\Delta t}\xi$, where $\xi \sim N(0,1)$ is a normally distributed random variable.

Suppose that, over time, the manager collects a percentage p of profits above a high water mark $H(t)$. The high water mark is the highest asset level reached, net of withdrawals, since initial investment. In particular, suppose that a manager collects a performance fee of $p \max(S(t) - H(t - \Delta t),0)$ at time $t \geq \Delta t$ then, the value of the manager's performance fee is equal to the value of p call options on $S(t)$ struck at $H(t)$. The value of the call can be expressed as the solution to a Black Scholes-type partial differential equation over some time horizon T.

For our purpose, it is not necessary to specify the precise value of the high water mark contract. However, we can use the Goetzmann, Ingersoll and Ross model to determine a manager's optimal use of leverage. Our leverage model is somewhat stylized. In our opinion, however, it captures a manager's typical response to varying asset levels. Suppose that we denote a fund's leverage by l and assume that l is capped by l_{max}. (Usually, a fund's offering documents set a strict limit on leverage.) If the manager's strategy is scalable, then $\mu = \mu(l)$, $\sigma = \sigma(l)$ increase linearly in l. This means that slippage does not increase as more capital is put to work. Since the high water mark gives the manager a long call position, the manager's expected profit should be increasing in μ and σ. Naively, a manager would want to maximize his leverage in order to make his expected payoff as large as possible.

This is a reasonable assumption whenever $S(t)$ is close to $H(t)$, since in this region the high water mark contract increases sharply as a function of volatility. However, a manager will typically lower his volatility at the extremes when $S(t)$ and $H(t)$ are far apart. When $S(t) \ll H(t)$, the fund may be close to liquidation. Although a manager would like to increase the expected value of his performance fee, he does not want to risk his regular management fee. Increasing leverage increases the probability of default; if this were to occur, the manager would no longer receive the percentage c.[5] When $S(t) \gg H(t)$, a manager may wish to lock in a profit for the year by reducing leverage and 'coasting'. It is widely known that many managers who are outperforming their return targets for a year

---

[5]Our anonymous referee has correctly pointed out that some managers will increase leverage when $S(t) \ll H(t)$, to increase the expected value of the performance fee. These tend to be small managers who need a large performance fee to stay in business. In our experience, however, funds with relatively large assets under management tend to take a conservative posture near the default zone. Thus, they decrease leverage when $S(t) \ll H(t)$. The liquidity haircut is larger than in our chapter, if we assume a manager will increase his leverage near default.

will coast. If they finish a year too far ahead of their stated target, investors may conclude that the fund manager is unable to accurately gauge the risk in his portfolio.

While Goetzmann, Ibbotson and Ross think of the incentive clause as a call option type structure, we prefer to compare it with a risky convertible bond. So long as a manager stays in business, he continues to receive the 'coupon' payment S. In the meantime, he can collect a performance fee according to whether p $\max(S(t) - H(t - \Delta t),0)$ is in the money. If the fund defaults, he collects nothing. We use a knockout barrier to model the probability of default. If, at any time t, $S(t)$ $< LH(t)$, where $0 < L < 1$ is a constant, then a large number of investors will withdraw and the fund will be forced to liquidate its positions. For example, if $L = 0.85$, then the fund will be forced to liquidate as soon as assets decline 15% from the high water mark. After liquidation, we further assume that the investor is only able to recover some percentage of $LH(t)$, say 50%.

For example, suppose that the high water mark is $100 million, the annual management fee is 1.5% and the performance fee is 20%. The manager's P&L profile and use of leverage are illustrated in the Graph given below. If the fund reaches the default threshold, we assume that the manager not only loses this year's performance fee, but also a performance fee for the next 3 years (we assume a discount rate of 0). Here, we have assumed that it will take some time for the manager to grow his assets to $100 million again.

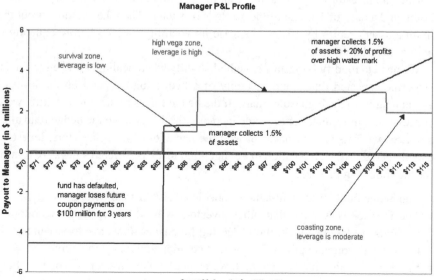

7.3   LONGSTAFF'S METHOD

Now that we have a picture of the hedge fund manager's strategy, we can study the appropriate rebalancing strategy for an investor. We want to know how much the investor should be compensated (in volatility terms) for his inability to move funds out of the hedge fund. Our approach is to use a variation of Longstaff's method (forthcoming).

Longstaff has developed a technique for calculating the illiquidity premium of an asset, such as a stock. The idea is to construct a portfolio consisting of a reference asset (e.g. a money market account) and the restricted asset. First, it is assumed that there are no liquidity constraints. This is the benchmark case. The investor tries to maximize his expected utility by rebalancing his portfolio over time, as necessary. Next, the investor is not allowed to transfer money between the liquid asset and the restricted one. Here, he chooses static weights to maximize the expected utility of his portfolio.

It is clear that the expected utility is at least as large in the case where the investor does not have any liquidity constraints. In general, it should be larger. We then ask, how much extra return should the restricted asset have to make the expected utility functions the same? According to Longstaff, this is the appropriate illiquidity premium. For example, suppose that the investor's utility function is a simple information ratio, such as

$$\frac{portfolio\ return}{portfolio\ volatility}.$$

Further, an investor is able to achieve an information ratio of 1.1 if both assets are liquid and a ratio of 1 if one of the assets is restricted. Then, he should haircut the illiquid asset's return by 10% or increase its volatility by 10% before equating it with a more liquid asset.

We need to modify Longstaff's method slightly when dealing with hedge funds, since the expected return and volatility of a hedge fund depend on the level of assets relative to the high water mark. If the hedge fund's return and volatility were constant over time, an investor would increase his allocation to the hedge fund after a drawdown. This is not consistent with the behavior of most investors. Investors usually decrease their allocation to a hedge fund that has suffered a negative return, for the following reasons:

- The hedge fund investment is now considered riskier than before.
- The investor is worried that other investors will withdraw. If the withdrawal amounts are large enough, the hedge fund manager may have to unwind positions at unfavourable prices. This would compound the negative return.
- Since most hedge funds have high water marks, the investor is worried about organizational risk. If the key employees in the fund do not believe they will get

reasonable bonuses for the next few years (bonuses are usually taken from the performance fee), they may leave.

We have incorporated investor behaviour into our model by using variable leverage and the knockout feature to model the evolution of a fund's assets over time.

Before we can apply a variant of Longstaff's method to a concrete example, we need to specify the investor's profit and loss function, as follows:

- If $S(t) \gg H(t)$, then the value of the investor's allocation is $(1 - p)(S(t) - H(t)) + H(t)$ and l (the strategy's leverage) is moderate. The manager is coasting, since there is only a small amount of vega in the management and performance contract. Thus, μ and σ are also moderate.
- If $S(t)$ is close to $H(t)$, then l is large, since the value of the incentive clause to the manager increases sharply in l. Here, vega is large and positive.
- If $S(t)$ is close to a threshold default level, then l is small, since the manager wants to continue to collect a percentage c of assets. As volatility increases, the probability of default increases sharply, and so the manager keeps l at a relatively low level. Vega is large and negative.
- If $S(t)$ drops below the default level, the fund liquidates. The value of the investor's allocation is then some fraction of the default level. In the example in the next section, we assume that the investors receive 50% of the threshold amount.

In our model, drift and volatility of assets are level-dependent and the leverage l is a step function in the argument $S(t) - H(t)$.

7.4 SIMULATING THE ILLIQUIDITY PREMIUM

In this section, we present a numerical example where an investor's illiquidity premium can be directly simulated, using Longstaff's method.

Suppose there is an investor who wants to invest in a hedge fund and a traditional mutual fund. The investor's utility function is specified by

$$\frac{portfolio\ return}{portfolio\ volatility}.$$

and he wishes to maximize his expected utility over a horizon of 2 years. Initially, the mutual fund and hedge fund have identical risk reward characteristics.

- The historical annual return and volatility of the mutual fund and hedge fund are 10% and 10%, respectively. We assume that the mutual fund returns evolve according to a random walk.
- The mutual fund and the hedge fund are uncorrelated.

However, for simplicity, we assume that the investor cannot move money in or out of the hedge fund over time.

In turn, the hedge fund manager varies his leverage according to the following schedule:

- The current level of assets is 100 (expressed in $ millions) and is equal to the current high water mark.
- The manager can vary his leverage once a month.
- If assets drop below 85, the fund liquidates and investors receive 50%, or 42.5. The manager loses his management fee. The number 85 is chosen because it is 1.5 standard deviations below the initial asset value, assuming moderate leverage.
- If assets rise above 110, the manager uses moderate leverage. His expected annual return is 10% with 10% volatility.
- If assets fall below 88.75 (75% of the way to default), the manager lowers his leverage (to half the moderate level). His expected annual return is 5% with 5% volatility.
- If assets are between 88.75 and 110, the manager uses maximal leverage, to increase the value of the high water mark contract. His expected annual return is 20% with 20% volatility.

We now create two sets of simulations, a benchmark set where the investor is allowed to rebalance once a month and another set where no rebalancing is allowed. In each case, we approximate the investors expected utility. We summarize the simulation results below.

7.4.1   Simulation 1 (monthly rebalancing)

The investor is aware of the manager's variable leverage and wants to maximize his expected utility over the next 2 years. At each time step, the manager's leverage is known. For example, at the start, the manager's assets are 100 so his expected return is 20% with 20% volatility. Thus, the investor initially optimizes his expected utility by allocating 67% to the traditional mutual fund and 33% to the hedge fund.

If, over time, the level of assets goes down, a more complicated calculation needs to be made. For example, if assets drop below 88.75 the expected return is 5%. However, the effective asset volatility is larger than 5%, since there is a positive probability of default at the next time step. We approximate the effective volatility by taking a probability weighted average, as follows.

Suppose that we are at time t and asset level $S(t)$. We know that $S(t + \Delta t) = S(t) + (\mu - c)S(t)\Delta t + \sigma S(t)\sqrt{\Delta t}\xi$ (assuming no withdrawals) and wish to calculate the probability that $S(t + \Delta t) \leq 85$, where $\Delta t = 0.083$ years. Solving for ξ, we find that this probability is the same as the probability p that

$$\xi \leq \frac{85 - S(t) - (\mu - c)S(t)\Delta t}{\sigma S(t)\sqrt{\Delta t}}$$

which can be calculated explicitly since $\xi \sim N(0,1)$. As the asset level moves close to default, p approaches 50%, assuming that the drift is 0. If

$$\xi \leq \frac{85 - S(t) - (\mu - c)S(t)\Delta t}{\sigma S(t)\sqrt{\Delta t}}$$

the fund defaults and we set

$$\xi = \frac{42.5 - S(t) - (\mu - c)S(t)\Delta t}{\sigma S(t)\sqrt{\Delta t}}$$

The volatility of $S(t)$ can then be approximated by $\sqrt{\mathrm{var}((1-p)\,\xi_1 + p\xi_2)}$, where $\xi_1 \sim N(0,\sigma^2)$ and

$$\xi_2 - N\left(\frac{42.5 - S(t) - (\mu - c)S(t)\Delta t}{\sigma S(t)\sqrt{\Delta t}}, 0\right)$$

We have simulated the investor's utility 40,000 times by calculating the realized annual return and volatility for each simulation. A histogram of information ratios appears in Figure 1. In the histogram, we have partitioned the *x*-axis in 0.025 increments. The expected utility over these simulations is 1.497.

7.4.2 Simulation 2 (no rebalancing)

In this case, we are not allowed to rebalance the portfolio for the entire 2 years. Beforehand, we do not know the optimal static allocation to the traditional fund

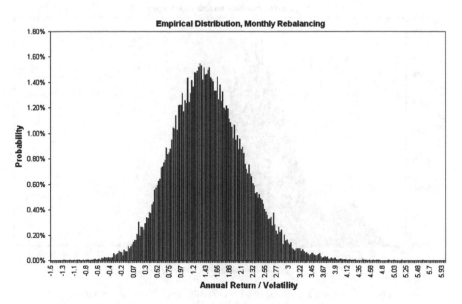

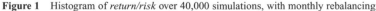

Figure 1   Histogram of *return/risk* over 40,000 simulations, with monthly rebalancing

and the hedge fund. By performing a separate simulation for different weights (in increments of 1%), we have found the optimal allocation to the traditional fund should be 55%, with 45% to the hedge fund. We can then plot the information ratio histogram in the same way as Simulation 1; the results appear in Figure 2.

Here, the distribution is clearly bimodal, since there is a much larger probability that the hedge fund will blow up before an investor can transfer funds to the traditional fund. The expected utility over 40,000 simulations is 1.347, or about 10% smaller than the benchmark case. We can either express the 10% difference as a return premium or in volatility terms. We choose the latter. Thus, the historical 10% volatility for the hedge fund should really be considered to be 11% (again, assuming moderate leverage).

In certain instances, we can use the liquidity haircut to decide how much we should allocate to a given hedge fund.

- As we have pointed out, it can be dangerous to characterize a hedge fund purely by its historical mean, variance and correlation with other funds. However, many fund of funds already use mean variance optimizers to make asset allocation decisions for traditional assets and are reluctant to develop entirely new models for alternatives. The result in this chapter provides a 'correction' term that can be applied before the optimization step.
- Fund of fund managers often make incremental changes to their portfolios using a ranking system. New funds are ranked according to a few summary statistics, such as historical mean, variance and maximum drawdown. When a change is

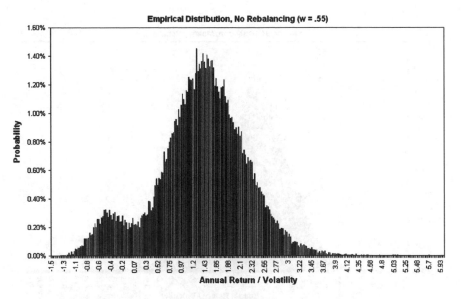

Figure 2   Histogram of *return/risk* over 40,000 simulations, no rebalancing

made, a new fund is chosen from the list. Our liquidity adjustment puts funds that trade in liquid markets (and usually have shorter lockups) on a more equal footing with funds that 'sell liquidity' for premium and should result in a different ranking from the one that relies purely on historical returns.

7.5 CONCLUSION

We have developed a technique for calculating the illiquidity haircut for a hedge fund. Since the lockup period and redemption schedules vary from fund to fund, the volatility adjustment in our numerical example should only be viewed as a guideline. Typically, funds that trade in more liquid markets (e.g. interest rate futures) offer more liquidity to an investor and should not be haircut as severely.

We have also made assumptions about the way, in which a hedge fund manager varies his leverage according to the level of assets in the fund. From experience, we have found that these assumptions are qualitatively correct. In a companion chapter, we develop a way to determine a hedge fund manager's optimal use of leverage more precisely.

REFERENCES

Fung, W. and Hseih, D. (1997) Survivorship bias and investment style in the returns of CTAs, *Journal of Portfolio Management*, **24**, 30–41.

Spurgin, R. and Schneeweis, T. (2000) A study of survival: commodity trading advisors, 1988–1996, *Journal of Alternative Investments*, (Winter).

Goetzmann, W., Ingersoll, J. and Ross, S. High water marks, working paper.

Longstaff, F. Optimal portfolio choice and the valuation of illiquid securities, *Review of Financial Studies*, forthcoming.

Chapter 8

Hedge fund investing: some words of caution

HARRY M. KAT[1]

ABSTRACT

In this chapter, we argue that proper hedge fund investing requires a much more elaborate approach to investment decision-making than currently in use by most investors. The available data on hedge funds should be corrected for various types of errors, survivorship and back-fill bias and autocorrelation. In addition, tools like mean-variance analysis and the Sharpe ratio are no longer appropriate when hedge funds are involved. Including hedge funds in a traditional investment portfolio can significantly improve that portfolio's mean-variance characteristics, but it can also be expected to lead to significantly lower skewness as well as higher kurtosis. This means that the case for hedge funds is a lot less straightforward than often suggested and requires investors to make a definite trade-off between profit and loss potential.

8.1 INTRODUCTION

Hedge funds have become very popular with institutional and especially high net worth investors. As a result, the amount of assets under management by hedge funds has grown from around $40 billion in 1990 to an estimated $900

---

[1]Professor of Risk Management, Cass Business School, City University, London.

billion in 2005. In line with this, the number of hedge funds worldwide has grown to around 8000. In the early days not much was known about hedge funds. Since 1994, however, a number of data vendors, hedge fund advisors and fund of funds operators have been collecting performance and other data on hedge funds. This has allowed researchers to take a more serious look at hedge funds. Of course, research in this area is still in its early days. However, it has become clear that hedge funds are a lot more complicated than common stocks and bonds and may not be as phenomenally attractive as many hedge fund managers and marketers want investors to believe. In this chapter, we will review some of the most important findings so far. From this it will become clear that hedge fund investing requires a much more elaborate approach than what most stock and bond investors are used to. Mechanically applying the same decision-making processes as typically used for stock and bond investing may lead to nasty surprises.

8.2   THE AVAILABLE DATA ON HEDGE FUNDS ARE FAR FROM PERFECT

With the industry still in its infancy and hedge funds under no formal obligation to disclose their results, gaining insight in the performance characteristics of hedge funds is not straightforward. Fortunately, many funds nowadays release performance as well as other administrative data to attract new and to accommodate existing investors. These data are collected by a number of data vendors and fund advisors, some of which make their data available to qualifying investors and researchers. Although better than nothing, the available data are not without problems though. Here are some of them:

- Most databases are of relatively low quality as most data vendors simply pass on the data supplied by the fund managers and their administrators without any independent verification. This means that before any serious research can take place, one must check the data for a number of possible errors and either correct these or delete the funds in question altogether.
- Most hedge funds only report into one or two databases. As a result, every database covers a different subset of the hedge fund universe and different researchers may arrive at quite different conclusions simply because different databases were used.
- Hedge fund databases tend to be backfilled, i.e. although typically funds only start reporting to a database some time after their actual start-up, when they do, their full track record is included in the database. Since only funds with good track records will eventually decide to report, this means that the available data sets are overly optimistic about hedge fund performance. As shown in Posthuma

and Van der Sluis (2003), on average actual hedge fund returns may be 4% per annum lower than reported.

- Most data vendors only supply data on funds that are still in operation. However, disappointing performance is a major reason for hedge funds to close down. As shown in Amin and Kat (2003), this means that the data available to investors will overestimate the returns that investors can realistically expect from investing in hedge funds by 2–4% per annum. In addition, concentrating on survivors only will lead investors to underestimate the risk of hedge funds by 10–20%.

- Since many hedge funds invest in illiquid assets, their administrators have great difficulty generating up-to-date valuations of their positions. When confronted with this problem, administrators either use the last reported transaction price or a conservative estimate of the current market price, which creates artificial lags in the evolution of these funds' net asset values. As shown in Brooks and Kat (2002), this will lead to very substantial underestimation of hedge fund risk, sometimes as high as 30–40%.

- Since most data vendors only started collecting data on hedge funds around 1994, the available data set on hedge funds is very limited. Apart from spanning a very short period of time, the available data on hedge funds also span a very special period: the bull market of the 1990s and the various crises that followed. This sharply contrasts with the situation for stocks and bonds. Not only do we have return data over differencing intervals much shorter than 1 month, we also have those data available over a period that extends over many business cycles. This has allowed us to gain insight into the main factors behind stock and bond returns and also allows us to distinguish between normal and abnormal market behaviour. The return generating process behind hedge funds on the other hand is still very much a mystery and so far we have little idea what constitutes normal behaviour and what not.

8.3   FUNDS FOLLOWING THE SAME TYPE OF STRATEGY MAY STILL BEHAVE VERY DIFFERENTLY

Hedge fund investment strategies tend to be quite different from the strategies followed by traditional money managers. In principle, every fund follows its own proprietary strategy, which means that hedge funds are an extremely heterogeneous group. It is common practice, however, to classify hedge funds depending on the main type of strategy that funds claim to follow. One popular classification is as follows:

Long/short equity: Funds that invest on both the long and the short side of the equity market. Unlike equity market neutral funds (see below), the portfolio may not always have zero market risk. Most funds have a long bias.

Equity market neutral: Funds that simultaneously take long and short positions of the same size within the same market, i.e. portfolios are designed to have zero market risk. Leverage is often applied to enhance returns.

Convertible arbitrage: Funds that buy undervalued convertible securities, while hedging (most of) the intrinsic risks.

Distressed securities: Funds that trade the securities of companies in reorganization and/or bankruptcy, ranging from senior secured debt to common stock.

Merger arbitrage: Funds that trade the securities of companies involved in a merger or acquisition, buying the stocks of the company being acquired while shorting the stocks of its acquirer.

Global macro: Funds that aim to profit from major economic trends and events in the global economy, typically large currency and interest rate shifts. These funds make extensive use of leverage and derivatives.

Emerging markets: Funds that focus on emerging and less mature markets. These funds tend to be long only because in many emerging markets short selling is not permitted and futures and options are not available.

Given the above classification, the question arises whether funds classified as following the same type of strategy indeed generate similar returns. We can easily investigate this by calculating the correlation between the returns of funds within each strategy group. Table 1 shows the average correlations between individual hedge funds belonging to the above strategy groups. From the diagonal we see that the average correlations between funds within the same strategy group are quite low. This makes it clear that although funds may be classified in the same strategy group, this does in no way mean that they will produce similar returns. The correlation coefficients between funds belonging to different strategy groups are low as well. The fact that the average correlation between funds of the same type and between different types of funds is of a similar order of magnitude is an interesting finding. It suggests that it might not make too much difference whether an investor diversifies within a given strategy group or between strategy groups.

Table 1   Average correlations between individual hedge funds 1994–2001

	MA	DS	EMN	CA	GM	L/S	EM
Merger arbitrage	**0.45**	0.30	−0.04	0.18	0.07	0.24	0.29
Distressed securities	0.30	**0.39**	0.18	0.28	0.15	0.32	0.14
Equity mkt. neutral	−0.04	0.18	**0.23**	0.09	0.03	−0.02	0.05
Convertible arbitrage	0.18	0.28	0.09	**0.28**	0.09	0.23	0.08
Global macro	0.07	0.15	0.03	0.09	**0.26**	0.09	0.10
Long/short equity	0.24	0.32	−0.02	0.23	0.09	**0.24**	0.27
Emerging markets	0.29	0.14	0.05	0.08	0.10	0.27	**0.52**

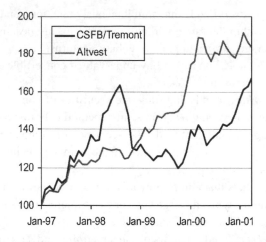

Figure 1   CSFB/Tremont and Altvest macro indices January 1997–May 2001

8.4   SIMILAR INDICES FROM DIFFERENT INDEX PROVIDERS MAY BEHAVE VERY DIFFERENTLY

Most data vendors use their databases to calculate one overall or aggregate index as well as a number of sub-indices, corresponding to the various types of hedge fund strategies mentioned earlier. Given the heterogeneity of each style group and the fact that different databases contain many different funds, however, one can expect substantial differences between indices that aim to cover the same type of strategy. Figure 1, for example, shows the evolution of the CSFB/Tremont and Altvest global macro indices over the period January 1997–May 2001. From the graph it is clear that both indices paint a completely different picture and that it is very well possible for one index to go up while at the same time the other index goes down.

Another way to see how different the available indices are is to calculate the correlation between the different hedge fund indices that claim to track the same strategy. The results for global macro can be found in Table 2. The low correlation coefficients confirm that there is considerable heterogeneity between these indices

Table 2   Correlations between global macro hedge fund indices 1994–2001

	HENNESSEE	HFR	CSFB/TREMONT	TUNA	ALTVEST	VAN
ZURICH	0.47	0.46	0.29	0.28	0.37	0.12
HENNESSEE		0.80	0.66	0.39	0.52	0.35
HFR			0.73	0.52	0.77	0.55
CSFB/TREMONT				0.52	0.50	0.35
TUNA					0.37	0.08
ALTVEST						0.51

despite the fact that they aim to reflect the same type of hedge fund strategy. In short, investors' perceptions of hedge fund performance and value added will heavily depend on the index studied.

8.5   THE TRUE RISKS OF HEDGE FUNDS TEND TO BE SERIOUSLY UNDERESTIMATED

Marking-to-market problems tend to create lags in the evolution of hedge funds' net asset values, which statistically shows up as autocorrelation in hedge funds returns. As discussed in Brooks and Kat (2002), this autocorrelation causes estimates of the standard deviation of hedge fund returns to exhibit a systematic downward bias. Table 3 shows the average autocorrelation found in the returns of individual hedge funds from the various strategy groups. The table shows that the problem is especially acute for convertible arbitrage and distressed securities funds, which makes sense as these funds' assets will typically be the most difficult to value. One way to correct for the observed autocorrelation is to 'unsmooth' the observed returns by creating a new set of returns, which are more volatile but whose other characteristics are unchanged. One method to do so stems from the real estate finance literature, where due to smoothing in appraisals and infrequent valuations of properties, the returns of direct property investment indices suffer from similar problems as hedge fund returns. Table 4 shows the average standard deviations of the original as well as the unsmoothed returns on individual hedge funds belonging to the different strategy groups. From the table we see that the difference between the observed and the true standard deviation can be very substantial. For distressed securities funds the true standard deviation is almost 30% higher than observed. For convertible arbitrage funds the difference is even higher.

A second reason why many investors think hedge funds are less risky than they really are results from the use of the standard deviation as the sole measure of risk. Generally speaking, risk is one word, but not one number. The returns on portfolios of stocks and bonds risk are more or less normally distributed. Because normal distributions are fully described by their mean and standard deviation, the risk of such

Table 3   Average 1-month autocorrelation individual hedge fund returns 1994–2001

	AC (1)
Merger arbitrage	0.13
Distressed securities	0.25
Equity mkt. neutral	0.08
Convertible arbitrage	0.30
Global macro	0.03
Long/short equity	0.09
Emerging markets	0.15

portfolios can indeed be measured with one number. Confronted with non-normal distributions, however, it is no longer appropriate to use the standard deviation as the sole measure of risk. In that case investors should also look at the degree of symmetry of the distribution, as measured by its so-called 'skewness', and the probability of extreme positive or negative outcomes, as measured by the distribution's 'kurtosis'. A symmetrical distribution will have a skewness equal to zero, while a distribution that implies a relatively high probability of a large loss (gain) is said to exhibit negative (positive) skewness. A normal distribution has a kurtosis of 3, while a kurtosis higher than 3 indicates a relatively high probability of a large loss or gain. Since most investors are in it for the longer run, they strongly rely on compounding effects. This means that negative skewness and high kurtosis are extremely undesirable features as one big loss may destroy years of careful compounding.

Table 5 shows the average skewness and kurtosis found in the returns of individual hedge funds from various strategy groups. From the table it is clear that hedge fund returns tend to be far from normally distributed and exhibit significant negative skewness as well as substantial kurtosis. Put another way, hedge fund returns may exhibit relatively low standard deviations but they also tend to provide skewness and kurtosis attributes that are exactly opposite to what investors desire. It is this whole package that constitutes hedge fund risk, not just the standard deviation.

Table 4   Average standard deviations original and unsmoothed individual hedge fund returns 1994–2001

	Original	Unsmoothed
Merger arbitrage	1.75	2.02
Distressed securities	2.37	3.05
Equity mkt. neutral	2.70	3.04
Convertible arbitrage	3.01	4.00
Global macro	5.23	5.37
Long/short equity	5.83	6.37
Emerging markets	8.33	9.75

Table 5   Average skewness and kurtosis individual hedge fund returns 1994–2001

	Skewness	Kurtosis
Merger arbitrage	−0.50	7.60
Distressed securities	−0.77	8.92
Equity mkt. neutral	−0.40	5.58
Convertible arbitrage	−1.12	8.51
Global macro	1.04	10.12
Long/short equity	0.00	6.08
Emerging markets	−0.36	7.83

8.6   SHARPE RATIOS AND ALPHAS OF HEDGE FUNDS CAN BE HIGHLY MISLEADING

To evaluate hedge fund performance many investors use the so-called Sharpe ratio, which is calculated as the ratio of the average excess return and the return standard deviation of the fund being evaluated. When applied to raw hedge fund return data, the relatively high means and low standard deviations offered by hedge funds lead to Sharpe ratios that are considerably higher than those of the relevant benchmark indices. Whilst this type of analysis is widely used, it is again not without problems. First, survivorship and backfill bias and autocorrelation will cause investors to overestimate the mean and underestimate the standard deviation. Second, the Sharpe ratio does not take account of the negative skewness and excess kurtosis observed in hedge fund returns. This means that the Sharpe ratio will tend to systematically overstate true hedge fund performance. In this context it is important to note that there tends to be a clear relationship between a fund's Sharpe ratio and the skewness and kurtosis of that fund's return distribution. High Sharpe ratios tend to go together with negative skewness and high kurtosis. This means that the relatively high mean and low standard deviation offered by hedge funds is not a free lunch. Investors simply pay for a more attractive Sharpe ratio in the form of more negative skewness and higher kurtosis.

Another performance measure often used is 'alpha'. The idea behind alpha is to first construct a portfolio that replicates the sensitivities of a fund to the relevant return generating factors and then compare the fund return with the return on that portfolio. If the fund produces a higher average return, this can be interpreted as superior performance since both share the same return generating factors. The main problem with this approach lies in the choice of return generating factors. As mentioned before, we have little idea what factors really generate hedge fund returns. As a result, investors that calculate hedge funds' alphas are likely to leave out one or more relevant risk factors. This will produce excess return where in reality there is none. Good examples of often forgotten but extremely important risks are credit and liquidity risk. So far, no study of hedge fund performance has correctly figured in credit or liquidity risk as a source of return, despite the fact that some hedge funds virtually live off it.

Providing liquidity to a market can be expected to be compensated by a higher average return. However, when this is not taken into account, we will find alpha where there is in fact none. Table 6 provides a simple example. For individual funds in the various strategy groups, Table 6 shows (a) the average alpha assuming the stock and bond market are the only relevant risk factors, and (b) the average autocorrelation coefficient found in these funds monthly returns. Since the autocorrelation found in hedge fund returns is primarily the result of marking-to-market problems in illiquid markets, we can use the autocorrelation coefficient as a

Table 6   Regression individual hedge fund alphas on autocorrelation
coefficients 1994–2001

	Average alpha	Average AC (1)	Regression coefficient
Merger arbitrage	1.20	0.13	1.1356
Distressed securities	0.89	0.25	0.8720
Equity mkt. neutral	0.40	0.08	0.3112
Convertible arbitrage	0.97	0.30	1.2975
Global macro	0.26	0.03	0.2864
Long/short equity	0.94	0.09	0.8954
Emerging markets	0.33	0.15	0.3680

measure of the liquidity risk taken on by a fund. From the table we see that there tends to be a positive relationship between alpha and autocorrelation. This is also confirmed by the last column, which shows the results of regressing the alphas of the funds in every strategy group on their respective autocorrelation coefficients. All regression coefficients are positive, meaning that in every category the funds that take more liquidity risk also tend to be the funds with the highest alphas.

The above makes it very clear that when it comes to hedge funds, traditional performance evaluation methods like the Sharpe ratio and alpha can be extremely misleading. A high Sharpe ratio or alpha should not be interpreted as an indication of superior manager skill, but first and foremost as an indication that further research is required. One can only speak of superior performance if such research shows that the manager in question generates the observed excess return without taking any unusual and/or catastrophic risks. Unfortunately, simply studying a manager's past returns will not be enough. Apart from the fact that most hedge fund managers do not have much of a track record to study, extreme events only occur infrequently so that it is hard if not impossible to identify the presence of catastrophic risk from a relatively small sample of returns. Consider the following example. A substantial portion of the outstanding supply of catastrophe-linked bonds are held by hedge funds. These bonds pay an exceptionally high coupon in return for the bondholder putting (part of) his principal at risk. Since the world has not seen a major catastrophe for some time now, these bonds have performed very well and the available return series show little skewness. However, this does not give an accurate indication of the actual degree of skewness as when a catastrophe does eventually occur, these bonds will produce very large losses.

8.7   THERE ARE NO SHORTCUTS IN HEDGE FUND SELECTION

When it comes to fund selection, the first thing that investors should (but hardly ever) do is to investigate how good one has to be in predicting future winners and losers to actually make a difference, i.e. to do significantly better than the index or a randomly selected portfolio of funds. Subsequently, investors should ask themselves how likely it is that they indeed possess the required degree of fund picking skills. Recent research by Martin (2001) has shown that the level of accuracy required to be a successful hedge fund picker is very, very high. Only investors that have an almost supernatural talent for distinguishing future winner and losers can expect to significantly outperform the average. This leaves us with the question how likely it is that an investor (and that includes fund of funds managers) indeed possesses such an extremely high level of skill.

Many investors allocate to different managers based on these managers' historical track record. Relatively good performance is rewarded with a high allocation, while badly performing managers are replaced. The weight given to a track record by investors implies that many believe that good and bad performance persists, i.e. that winners will continue to win and losers will continue to lose. Unfortunately, this is not the case. Table 7 shows the results of a regression of average individual hedge fund returns over the period June 1994–November 1997 on average individual hedge fund returns over the period December 1997–May 2001. The regression coefficients are all insignificant, pointing at a complete lack of persistence in these hedge funds' returns.

A strategy of allocating only to top performers can not be expected to yield a significantly higher return, but what about other strategies like only investing in young funds, large funds, funds where the manager has a PhD, funds that charge extremely high fees, etc.? So far, after properly controlling for all the risks involved, none of these strategies has turned out to produce superior results. At first sight it often appears that on average small, young funds produce higher returns than larger, older funds. There are several good reasons for this, however. First, most funds do not start contributing to a database until some time after their actual start-up date. This means that we have no information available about funds that close down before entering a database, which will lead us to overestimate the average return on young funds. Second, young funds are more risky. They are more likely to close down due to lack of assets under management or disappointing performance. In addition, successful young funds will have to undergo significant organizational changes to deal with the increase of assets under management and the greater variety in investment strategies followed. This makes them more risky in operational terms as well.

Table 7 Regression mean 1994–1997 on mean 1997–2001

	Coefficient	t-statistic	R^2
Long/short equity	0.1815	1.5698	0.0217
Merger arbitrage	0.2584	1.6175	0.0439
Global macro	−0.7999	−1.9220	0.1976
Emerging markets	0.3031	2.1496	0.1614
Equity market neutral	0.0898	0.4960	0.0084

Another indication of the difficulty of selecting future winners and losers can be found in the performance of funds of hedge funds. Over the period 1994–2001, an equally weighted portfolio of randomly selected hedge funds would have offered an almost 3% higher mean return than the average fund of funds. Since this is more or less equal to the annual management and incentive fee charged by fund of funds, this strongly suggests that the timing and fund picking activities of the average fund of funds manager are not rewarded by a higher return.

The above strongly suggests that, at least for the majority of investors, successful fund picking is an illusion. Frantically chasing winners, as so many investors and funds of funds seem to do nowadays, can only be expected to lead to higher costs and therefore lower bottom-line returns. A much more rational strategy is to develop proper due diligence and monitoring procedures, use these to identify professional, trustworthy managers (that charge reasonable fees) and simply stick with them.

8.8   HEDGE FUND DIVERSIFICATION IS NOT A FREE LUNCH

The only time when investors should not diversify is when they have substantial fund picking skills. Since this is quite unlikely when it comes to hedge funds, hedge fund investors should always invest in a diversified basket of funds and not in just one or two individual funds. For risk-averse investors, diversification is often said to be the only true free lunch in finance. Unfortunately, this does not include hedge funds. Although combining hedge funds into a basket will substantially reduce the standard deviation of the return on that portfolio, it can also be expected to lower the skewness and raise the correlation with the stock market.

Table 8 shows the standard deviation, skewness and correlation with the S&P 500 of the average individual hedge fund in the various strategy groups as well as an equally weighted portfolio of all funds in each group. From the table we see that forming portfolios leads to a very substantial reduction in standard deviation. With

Table 8   Individual hedge fund and hedge fund portfolio risks

	Individual hedge funds			Portfolio of hedge funds		
	Standard deviation	Skewness	Corr. S&P 500	Standard deviation	Skewness	Corr. S&P 500
Merger arbitrage	1.75	−0.50	0.47	1.04	−2.19	0.56
Distressed securities	2.37	−0.77	0.37	1.54	−2.60	0.47
Equity mkt. neutral	2.70	−0.40	0.07	1.14	−0.41	0.19
Convertible arbitrage	3.01	−1.12	0.19	1.64	−1.35	0.38
Global macro	5.23	1.04	0.14	2.43	0.87	0.37
Long/short equity	5.83	0.00	0.35	2.95	−0.29	0.63
Emerging markets	8.33	−0.36	0.44	6.15	−0.65	0.67

the exception of emerging market funds, the portfolio standard deviations are approximately half the standard deviations of the average individual fund. This again signals that the degree of correlation between funds in the same strategy group must be quite low. Contrary to standard deviation, skewness is not diversified away and actually drops further as portfolios are formed. With the exception of equity market neutral funds, the portfolio skewness figures are lower than for the average individual fund, with especially merger arbitrage and distressed securities funds standing out. Despite the lack of overall correlation, it appears that when things are bad for one fund, they tend to be bad for other funds in the same sector as well. Finally, comparing the correlation on individual funds and portfolios we see clearly that the returns on portfolios of hedge funds tend to be much more correlated with the stock market than the returns on individual funds. Although individual hedge funds may be more or less market neutral, the portfolios that most investors invest in are not.

8.9   HEDGE FUNDS DO NOT COMBINE VERY WELL WITH EQUITY

It is often argued that given their relatively weak correlation with other asset classes, hedge funds can play an important role in risk reduction and yield enhancement strategies. This diversification service does not come for free, however. Although the inclusion of hedge funds in a portfolio may significantly improve that portfolio's mean-variance characteristics, it can also be expected to lead to significantly lower skewness as well as higher kurtosis. Table 9 shows what happens to the standard deviation, skewness and kurtosis of the portfolio return distribution if, starting with 50% stocks and 50% bonds, we introduce hedge fund in a traditional stock-bond portfolio. As expected, when hedge funds are introduced the standard deviation drops significantly. This represents the relatively low

Table 9   Effects of combining hedge funds with stocks and bonds

% HF	SD	Skewness	Kurtosis
0	2.49	−0.33	2.97
5	2.43	−0.40	3.02
10	2.38	−0.46	3.08
15	2.33	−0.53	3.17
20	2.29	−0.60	3.28
25	2.25	−0.66	3.42
30	2.22	−0.72	3.58
35	2.20	−0.78	3.77
40	2.18	−0.82	3.97
45	2.17	−0.85	4.19
50	2.16	−0.87	4.41

correlation of hedge funds with stocks and bonds. This is the good news. The bad news, however, is that a similar drop is observed in the skewness of the portfolio return. In addition, we also observe a rise in kurtosis.

Especially the skewness effect goes far beyond what one might expect given the hedge fund skewness results in Table 5. When things go wrong in the stock market, they also tend to go wrong for hedge funds. Not necessarily because of what happens to stock prices (after all, many hedge funds do not invest in equity), but because a significant drop in stock prices will often be accompanied by a widening of credit spreads, a significant drop in market liquidity, higher volatility, etc. Since hedge funds are highly sensitive to such factors, when the stock market drops, hedge funds can be expected to show relatively bad performance as well. Recent experience provides a good example. Over the year 2002, the S&P 500 dropped by more than 20% with relatively high volatility and substantially widening credit spreads. Distressed debt funds, at the start of 2002 seen by many investors as one of the most promising sectors, suffered substantially from the widening of credit spreads. Credit spreads also had a negative impact on convertible arbitrage funds. Stock market volatility worked in their favour, however. Managers focusing on volatility trading generally fared best, while managers actively taking credit exposure did worst. Equity market neutral funds suffered greatly from a lack of liquidity, while long/short equity funds with low net exposure outperformed managers that remained net long throughout the year. As a result, overall hedge fund performance in 2002 as measured by the main hedge fund indices was more or less flat.

8.10   MODERN PORTFOLIO THEORY IS TOO SIMPLISTIC TO DEAL WITH HEDGE FUNDS

Implicitly or explicitly, many investors evaluate and select investment portfolios in the mean-variance framework of Markowitz (1959), which formalizes the idea that out of all possible portfolios a risk-averse investor will only be interested in those portfolios that offer the highest expected return for a given level of standard deviation. When studied in the mean-variance framework, the inclusion of hedge funds in a portfolio appears to pay off impressive dividends. However, since mean-variance analysis only looks at the mean and standard deviation, it skips over the fact that with hedge funds more attractive mean-variance attributes tend to go hand in hand with less attractive skewness and kurtosis properties.

We performed two standard mean-variance optimisations; one with only stocks and bonds and one with stocks, bonds and hedge funds as the available asset classes. The results of both optimizations can be found in Table 10. Starting with the case without hedge funds (top panel), we see that moving upwards over the efficient frontier results in a straightforward exchange of bonds for stocks. Since stocks have a higher mean than bonds, the mean goes up. While this happens, the skewness of

Table 10 Mean-variance optimal portfolios

Std. Dev.	Stocks and bonds only					
	Mean	% Stocks	% Bonds	% Hfund	Skew	Kurtosis
2	0.77	32.79	67.21		0.04	3.23
2.5	0.95	50.31	49.69		−0.34	2.97
3	1.10	64.68	35.32		−0.55	3.24
3.5	1.23	77.86	22.14		−0.68	3.57
4	1.36	90.44	9.56		−0.77	3.86
	Stocks, bonds and hedge funds					
2	0.92	18.07	26.81	55.12	−0.82	4.39
2.5	1.06	29.95	10.75	59.30	−0.99	5.26
3	1.20	45.07	0	54.93	−1.07	5.47
3.5	1.30	67.08	0	32.92	−1.00	4.81
4	1.39	86.14	0	13.86	−0.89	4.32

the return distribution drops in a more or less linear fashion as stock returns are more negatively skewed than bond returns. The kurtosis of the return distribution remains more or less unchanged. Next, we added hedge funds and recalculated the efficient frontier (bottom panel). Moving over the efficient frontier, we see that at first bonds are exchanged for stocks while the hedge fund allocation remains more or less constant. When the bond allocation is depleted, the equity allocation continues to grow but now at the expense of the hedge fund allocation. Similar to the case without hedge funds, if we increase the standard deviation, the mean goes up, while the skewness of the return distribution goes down. Unlike what we saw before, however, skewness drops as long as bonds are being replaced by equity but rises again as hedge funds start to be replaced by equity. The lowest level of skewness is reached when the bond allocation reaches 0%, which is fully in line with our earlier observation that in terms of skewness hedge funds and equity are not a good mix.

Comparing the case with and without hedge funds we see a significant improvement in the mean, especially for lower standard deviations. However, we also see a major deterioration in skewness and kurtosis, with the largest change taking pace exactly there where the mean improves most. From this it is painfully clear that standard mean-variance portfolio decision-making is no longer appropriate when hedge funds are involved as it completely ignores these effects. When hedge funds are involved investors need a decision-making framework that also incorporates the skewness and kurtosis of the portfolio return distribution. Academic researchers have briefly worked on this kind of models in the early 1970s but, due to their higher level of complexity and because the returns on portfolios of stocks and bonds tend to be more or less normally distributed, none of them has attracted the kind of following that mean-variance models have.

8.11 ONE HAS TO INVEST AT LEAST 20% IN HEDGE FUNDS FOR IT TO MAKE A DIFFERENCE

Diversification is about not putting all of one's eggs in one basket. The idea, however, is not to put one egg in one basket and the other 99 in another. To fully realize the potential of diversification investors have to spread their portfolio over the various asset classes in a more or less equal fashion. This is also the picture that emerges from Table 9. Allocating 5% or 10% to hedge funds changes very little. Only if we invest 20% or more in hedge funds do we see significant changes in the standard deviation, skewness and kurtosis. The above observation may seem very obvious, but it appears to be largely forgotten by (potential) hedge fund investors, many of whom (are contemplating to) invest only between 1% and 5% in this asset class.

8.12 CONCLUSION

Proper hedge fund investing requires a much more elaborate approach to investment decision-making than currently in use by most investors. The available data on hedge funds should not be taken at face value, but should first be corrected for various types of errors, survivorship and backfill bias and autocorrelation. Tools like mean-variance analysis and the Sharpe ratio that many investors have become accustomed to over the years are no longer appropriate when hedge funds are involved as they concentrate on the good part while completely skipping over the bad part of the hedge fund story. Investors also have to find a way to figure in the long lock-up and advance notice periods, which make hedge fund investments highly illiquid. In addition, investors will have to give weight to the fact that without more insight in the way in which hedge funds generate their returns it is very hard to say something sensible about hedge funds' future longer run performance. The academic tools to accomplish this formally are not there (yet), meaning that more than ever investors will have to rely on good old-fashioned common sense.

It has also become clear that hedge funds are not the miracle cure that many investors think or have been told they are. Hedge funds offer investors a way to obtain a lower standard deviation and/or higher expected return but at the cost of a higher probability of a large loss, i.e. lower skewness and higher kurtosis. Whether the resulting portfolio makes for a more attractive investment than the original is purely a matter of taste, not a general rule. Finally, all those investors that (plan to) invest only 1–5% in hedge funds should seriously consider whether this is really worth the effort as such a small allocation will have very little effect on the performance of the overall portfolio. To make a real difference one has to allocate at least 20% to hedge funds.

REFERENCES

Amin, G. and Kat, H. (2003) Welcome to the dark side: hedge fund attrition and survivorship bias 1994–2001, *Journal of Alternative Investments*, Summer, 57–73.

Brooks, C. and Kat, H. (2002) The statistical properties of hedge fund index returns and their implications for investors, *Journal of Alternative Investments*, Fall, 26–44.

Markowitz, H. (1959) *Portfolio Selection: Efficient Diversification of Investments*, Wiley, New York.

Martin, G. (2001) Making sense of hedge fund returns: what matters and what doesn't, Working Paper Center for International Securities and Derivatives Markets, University of Massachusetts.

Posthuma, N. and Van der Sluis, P. (2003) A reality check on hedge fund returns, Working Paper ABP Investments.

Chapter 9

On ranking schemes and portfolio selection

MASSIMO DI PIERRO AND JACK W. MOSEVICH

ABSTRACT

There are now in use several risk-return indicators, which are utilized to rank historical returns of portfolios. Some popular ones are the Sharpe Ratio, the Sortino Ratio, Omega and the Stutzer Index, among others. It is well known that portfolio log-returns, especially of alternative assets, are not normally (Gaussian) distributed. This is the reason for the development of indicators other than the Sharpe Ratio. The purpose of this paper is to evaluate the relationships between these indicators for both Gaussian and non-Gaussian distributions. We prove mathematically that rankings are essentially the same for these indicators in a Gaussian environment, and different in a non-Gaussian one, which is as it should be. We are able to compute an implied utility function for the indicators and find that it is the same for all of them, something not very intuitive. We then propose a utility function, which corresponds more with what we expect investors to desire. We conclude by showing how to relate our results to the Markowitz MPT.

9.1 INTRODUCTION

In this paper we discuss different criteria for ranking portfolios including the Sharpe ratio (Sharpe, 1964), the Sortino ratio (Sortino and Van Der Meer, 1991; Sortino and Price, 1994; Sortino and Forsey, 1996), the kappa ratio (Kaplan and Knowles, 2004), the omega ratio (Shadwick and Keating, 2002; Sortino, 2001; Wilmott, 2000) and the Stutzer index (Amenc, Malaise, Martellini and Vaisse). We prove that in a world where portfolio returns are Gaussian distributions, all of the above ranking systems are equivalent in the sense that although they produce different numbers they will produce the same ranking order. We also prove that all of the above ranking systems implicitly assume a non-natural utility function that attributes the same utility to any positive return (utility equals to +1) and to all negative returns (utility equals to −1).

We propose a more natural utility function from which we derive a different ranking system for Gaussian portfolios that is not equivalent to the Sharpe ratio or any of the other rankings considered. Using the Berry–Esseen theorem we prove that our ranking system, embodied in equation (24), is applicable to portfolios with non-Gaussian returns under the condition that one plans to hold the portfolio for a sufficiently long time.

Finally we show how to apply our findings to Markowitz' Modern Portfolio Theory (Markowitz, 1952; Wilmott, 2000).

9.2   CONVENTIONS AND DEFINITIONS

Given a portfolio A whose historic values are $\{S_i\}$ we will indicate with $p(x) : R \rightarrow R^*$ the probability mass function of each of the random variables $x_i = \log(S_{i+1}/S_i)$. The probability mass function is normalized to 1. We also define as $F(x) = \int_{-\infty}^{x} p(z)\mathrm{d}z$ the usual cumulative distribution.

Throughout this paper we will also assume that r is the risk-free interest rate.

Definition: (*Ranking*). We define a raking as a functional $R(p) : R \times R^* \rightarrow R$ that maps the probability mass function p associated to a portfolio into a real number.

Definition: (*Equivalence*). We say that two rankings R_1 and R_2 are equivalent in a domain D if there exists a monotonic increasing function h such that for every probability mass function p in the domain D, $R_1(p) = h(R_2(p))$.

If two rankings are equivalent we will use the notation

$$R_1 \sim R_2$$

The equivalence relation as defined is symmetric and transitive.

Definition: (*Sharpe ratio*). Given a portfolio characterized by a probability mass function $p(x)$ the Sharpe (1964) ratio is defined as

$$R_{\text{Sharpe}}(p) \overset{\text{def}}{=} \frac{\mu - r}{\sigma} \tag{1}$$

where

$$\mu = \int_{-\infty}^{+\infty} x p(x)\mathrm{d}x \tag{2}$$

$$\sigma = \sqrt{\int_{-\infty}^{+\infty} (x - \mu)^2 \, p(x) \, \mathrm{d}x} \tag{3}$$

Herein we denote the Sharpe ratio by y, with no explicit reference to the risk-free rate r. Note that in the equations which follow, the letter r can also represent a minimal acceptable return.

Definition: (*Sortino ratio*). Given a portfolio characterized by a probability mass function $p(x)$ the Sortino ratio (Sortino and Van Der Meer, 1991; Sortino and Price, 1994; Sortino and Forsey, 1996) is defined as

$$R_{\text{Sortino}}(p) \stackrel{\text{def}}{=} \frac{\mu - r}{\sqrt{\int_{-\infty}^{r} (r - x)^2 \, p(x) \, dx}} \tag{4}$$

Definition: (*Kappa-n ratio*). Given a portfolio characterized by a probability mass function $p(x)$ the kappa ratio (Kaplan and Knowles, 2004) is defined as

$$R_{\text{kappa}-n}(p) \stackrel{\text{def}}{=} \frac{\mu - r}{\left[\int_{-\infty}^{r} (r - x)^n p(x) dx \right]^{1/n}} \tag{5}$$

Note that for $n = 2$, $R_{\text{kappa}-2}(p, r) \equiv R_{\text{Sortino}}(p, r)$.

Definition: (*Omega ratio*). Given a portfolio characterized by a probability mass function $p(x)$ the omega ratio (Shadwick and Keating, 2002; Sortino, 2001; Wilmott) is defined as

$$R_{\text{Omega}}(p) \stackrel{\text{def}}{=} \frac{\int_{\infty}^{r} (1 - F(x)) dx}{\int_{-\infty}^{r} F(x) dx} \tag{6}$$

Definition: (*Stutzer index*). Given a portfolio characterized by a probability mass function $p(x)$ the Stutzer index (Amenc, Malaise, Martellini and Vaisse) is defined as

$$R_{\text{Stutzer}}(p) \stackrel{\text{def}}{=} \lim_{T \to \infty} \frac{-\log F(rT)}{T} \tag{7}$$

The Stutzer index ranks portfolios according to the speed with which the probability of a negative return (when compared with rT) tends to zero when time grows ($T \to \infty$).

9.3 EQUIVALENCE IN A GAUSSIAN WORLD

In this section we will restrict to only domain

$$D = \left\{ p \, | \, p(x) = p_{\text{Gaussian}}(x) = \frac{1}{\sqrt{2\pi}\sigma} e^{-(x-\mu)^2/2\sigma^2} \right\} \tag{8}$$

portfolios having a Gaussian distributions of returns.

Theorem 1. $R_{\text{Sortino}} \sim R_{\text{Sharpe}}$.
  Proof. By explicit integration[1]

$$R_{\text{Sortino}}(p) = h_1(R_{\text{Sharpe}}(p))$$

Where

$$h_1(y) = \frac{\sqrt{2}y}{\sqrt{1 - \sqrt{2/\pi}e^{-y^2/2}y + y^2 - (1 + y^2)\,\text{erf}(y/\sqrt{2})}} \tag{9}$$

Recall that $y = (\mu - r)/\sigma$ is the Sharpe ratio. Since $h_1'(y) > 0$ for every finite real is y proves the equivalence.

Figure 1 shows a plot of h_1 and h_1'. It also shows that compared with the Sharpe ratio, the Sortino is relatively sensitive to changes of y for large values of y, but it becomes insensitive to y for negative values of y.

Theorem 2. $R_{\text{kappa}-n} \sim R_{\text{Sharpe}}$ for every n.
  Proof. By explicit integration

$$R_{\text{kappa}-n}(p) = h_2(R_{\text{Sharpe}}(p)) \tag{10}$$

$$h_2(y) = \frac{\pi^{1/(2n)}y}{\left[2^{(n-2)/2}e^{-y^2/2}g(y)\right]^{1/n}}$$

$$g(y) = \Gamma\left(\frac{1+n}{2}\right)\,{}_1F_1\left(\frac{1+n}{2}, \frac{1}{2}, y^2/2\right) - \sqrt{2}y_1F_1\left(\frac{1+n}{2}, \frac{3}{2}, y^2/2\right)$$

and $_1F_1(a, b, x)$ is a member of the family of hypergeometric functions. $h_2'(y) > 0$ for every even integer n and every finite real y. Figure 2 shows a plot of h_2 and h_2' for $n = 1, 2, 3$. It also shows how the K_n ratio exhibits the same sensitivity to y as the Sortino does, but the higher the value of n, the lower the sensitivity to y.

Theorem 3. $R_{\text{Omega}} \sim R_{\text{Sharpe}}$.
  Proof. By explicit integration

$$R_{\text{Omega}}(p) = h_3(R_{\text{Sharpe}}(p)) \tag{11}$$

$$h_3(y) = 1 + \frac{2y}{\sqrt{2/\pi}e^{-y^2/2} - y + y\,\text{erf}(y/\sqrt{2})}$$

$h_3'(y) > 0$ for finite real y. Figure 3 shows a plot of h_3 and h_3'.

---

[1] $\text{erf}(z) \overset{\text{def}}{=} \frac{2}{\sqrt{\pi}}\int_0^z e^{-x^2}\,dx$

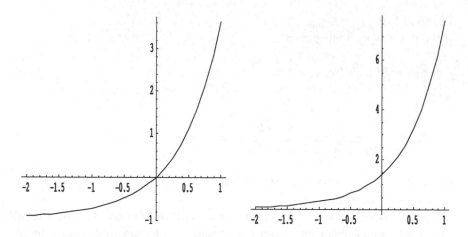

Figure 1 Plot of $h_1(y)$ (left) and $h_1'(y)$ (right). h_1 is the Sortino ratio as function of the Sharpe ratio for a portfolio with Gaussian returns

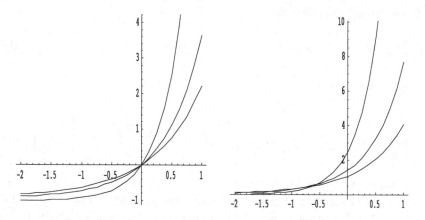

Figure 2 Plot of $h_2(y)$ (left) and $h_2'(y)$ (right) for $n = 1, 2, 3$

Theorem 4. $R_{\text{Stutzer}} \sim R_{\text{Sharpe}}$ if and only if $y > 0$.

Proof. By explicit integration

$$R_{\text{Stutzer}}(p) = h_4(R_{\text{Sharpe}}(p))$$

$$h_4(y) = \begin{cases} y^2/2 & \text{for } y > 0 \\ 0 & \text{for } y \leq 0 \end{cases} \tag{12}$$

$h_4'(y) > 0$ for real $y > 0$. Figure 4 shows a plot of h_4 and h_4'. For a portfolio with Gaussian mass function, the Stutzer index is unable to rank portfolios with negative y.

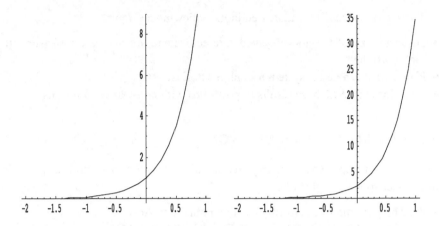

Figure 3   Plot of $h_3(y)$ (left) and h_3' (right). h_3 is the omega ratio as function of the Sharpe ratio for a portfolio with Gaussian returns

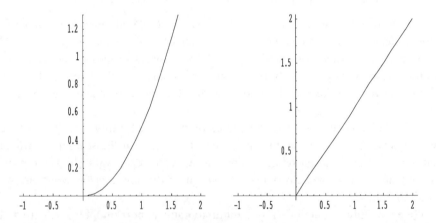

Figure 4   Plot of $h_4(y)$ (left) and h_4' (right). h_4' is the Stutzer index as function of the Sharpe ratio for a portfolio with Gaussian returns

So far, we have shown how in the domain of portfolios with Gaussian returns

$$R_{\text{Sharpe}} \sim R_{\text{Sortino}} \sim R_{\text{Kappa}-\text{n}} \sim R_{\text{Omega}} \tag{13}$$

and in the subdomain with portfolios with positive R_{Sharpe}

$$R_{\text{Sharpe}} \sim R_{\text{Stutzer}} \tag{14}$$

Moreover, we have shown how these indices tend to be more and more sensitive to y and for larger positive y and less and less sensitive for more negative y.

Three questions will be addressed in the following sections:

- Given that all of the above systems are equivalent, are they good measures to rank portfolios?
- If not, what is a better system to rank portfolios?
- How do we extend these results to portfolios with non-Gaussian returns?

9.4   RANKING AND RISK AVERSION

Consider a situation where the risk-free interest rate is $r = 5\%$ and four possible future scenarios for a portfolio:

- #1: The portfolio out-performs r with a return $x = 20\%$
- #2: The portfolio out-performs r with a return of $x = 10\%$
- #3: The portfolio under-performs r with a return of $x = 3\%$
- #4: The portfolio under-performs r with a return of $x = -2\%$.

It is clear that we prefer #1 to #2, #2 to #3 and #3 to #4 but how do we quantify this preference? How much more do we prefer #1 to #3 when compared to #2? How bad is #4 when compared with #3? The answers to these questions have nothing to do with probability (we are not discussing here the likelihood of one scenario over the other) but have to do with subjective choice and one's perception of risk.

This choice is equivalent to the choice of an implied utility function that we will indicate by $W(x)$. It returns one's subjective utility of the scenario in which the portfolio has a fixed return x. For logical reasons, we value higher returns more than lower returns. So $W'(x) \geq 0$ and this is the only *a priori* condition we wish to impose.

Given a utility function it is natural to rank a portfolio by evaluating a weighted average of $W(x)$ over all possible future scenarios. The weight factor is the probability of a future scenario with return x. This induced ranking can be expressed as

$$R_W(p) \overset{\text{def}}{=} \int_{-\infty}^{+\infty} W(x)p(x)\, \mathrm{d}x \tag{15}$$

Now the question becomes: in a Gaussian world, which choice of $W(x)$ produces a ranking equivalent to the Sharpe ratio (and all the other rankings equivalent to the Sharpe ratio)?

Surprisingly, the answer is

$$W(x) = W_{\text{naive}}(x) \overset{\text{def}}{=} (x - r)/|x - r| \tag{16}$$

which implies

$$R_{\text{naive}}(x) = \int_{-\infty}^{+\infty} W_{\text{naive}}(x) p(x) \, dx$$

$$= \int_{-\infty}^{+\infty} \frac{(x - r)e^{-(x-\mu)^2/2\sigma^2}}{|x - r| \sqrt{2\pi}\sigma} \, dx$$

$$= \text{erf}((\mu - r)/\sigma\sqrt{2})) \tag{17}$$

and

$$R_{\text{naive}}(p) = h_5(R_{\text{Sharpe}}(p)) \tag{18}$$

$$h_5(y) = \text{erf}(y/\sqrt{2})$$

We just proved that for portfolios with Gaussian returns $h_5'(y) > 0$.

Theorem 1. $R_{\text{naive}} \sim R_{\text{Sharpe}}$.

This finding is surprising because it implies that in a Gaussian world, ranking portfolios according to the Sharpe ratio, the Sortino, the Kappa, the Omega or the Stutzer index is equivalent to having the utility function in equation (16). This utility function is plotted in Figure 5.

W_{naive} is not a risk averse utility function. Referring to the examples of the four scenarios at the beginning of the section this naive utility function implies that we like scenarios #1 and #2 equally (utility $W = +1$) and we dislike scenarios #3 and #4 equally (utility $W = -1$).

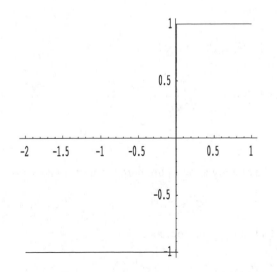

Figure 5   Plot of $W_{\text{naive}}(x)$, the utility function (function of the portfolio return) that is equivalent to ranking portfolios using the Sharpe ratio

9.5 A BETTER UTILITY FUNCTION

Clearly, the utility function induced by the Sharpe ratio is not natural and does not capture the natural risk aversion of many investors. There is an extensive literature in economics describing more rational choices for utility functions. Because this is a subjective choice we cannot claim that any one utility function is better than all others, but we can select a utility function that is more natural than the one in equation (16) and exhibits the following desirable characteristics:

- $W'(x) > 0$; the higher the return of a given scenario the higher the utility of the scenario.
- $W(r) = 0$; a scenario in which the return is the same as the risk-free rate has zero utility.
- $\lim_{x \to \infty} W'(x) = 0$; we became insensitive to x for large positive returns.
- $\lim_{x \to -\infty} W'(x) = \infty$; we are extremely sensitive to x for large negative returns.

A utility function that exhibits all of the above characteristics is the constant absolute risk aversion (CARA) (Wilmott)

$$W_{\text{CARA}}(x) \overset{\text{def}}{=} -e^{-m(x-r)} \tag{19}$$

Here k is a subjective number that measures one's risk aversion. The larger the k, the more risk averse one is. The CARA utility function $W_{\text{CARA}}(x)$, is shown in Figure 6.

When we substitute equation (19) into equation (15) for a Gaussian $p(x)$ we obtain

$$R_{\text{CARA}}(p) = \int_{-\infty}^{+\infty} W_{\text{CARA}}(x) p(x) \, dx \tag{20}$$

$$= \int_{-\infty}^{+\infty} -e^{m(r-x)} \frac{e^{-\frac{(x-\mu)^2}{2\sigma^2}}}{\sqrt{2\pi}\,\sigma} \, dx \tag{21}$$

$$= -e^{m(r-\mu)+m^2\sigma^2/2} \tag{22}$$

In order to have the ranking to be a pure number in the range $(-\infty, +\infty)$, we define

$$R_{\text{best}}(p) \overset{\text{def}}{=} \mu/r - 1 - m\sigma^2/(2r) \tag{23}$$

which is equivalent to $R_{\text{CARA}}(p)$ because

$$R_{\text{best}}(p) = h_6(R_{\text{CARA}}(p)) \tag{24}$$

$$h_6(z) = -\log(-z)/(mr) \tag{25}$$

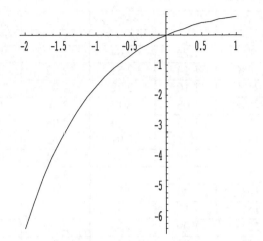

Figure 6   Plot of $W_{CARA}(x)$, the CARA utility function used to derive $R_{best}(p) \sim R_{CARA}(p)$

and $h'_6(z) > 0$ for $mr > 0$ and $z < 0$.

Note that, for the risk-free asset, $R_{best} \simeq 0$. "Good" portfolios rank above 0 and "bad" portfolios rank below 0.

It is important to notice how the Sharp ratio, as well as the Sortino, the kappa, the omega and the Stutzer index do not depend on any subjective parameters except for minimal acceptable return r (and n in the case of kappa), while Equation (23) depends also on the subjective value of m. This is not surprising since the latter incorporates a scale, represented by m, that encodes information about how better scenario #1 is when compared with scenario #2. The Sharpe ranking does not incorporate any information about this scale and it assumes that scenario #1 is as good as scenario #2, and scenario #3 is as bad as scenario #4. The introduction of at least one parameter (in our case m) is necessary to quantify the cost of taking a risk. The higher the value of m the higher will be the cost of risk.

The ranking scheme R_{best} is not equivalent to R_{Sharpe} as shown for the following portfolios (Gaussian returns, $r = 5\%$ and $m = 2, 4, 8$, the latter choices will be explained later).

Note that in all the schemes portfolio, E ranks better than A (because it has the same risk but higher return) and I (because it has the same return but lower risk). For the same reasons F ranks better than B and J, G than C and K, and H than D and L as was expected. Nevertheless, the relative ranking of portfolios is different for different schemes and different choices of m:

- $R_{Sharpe} \Rightarrow$ E, A, F, I, G, B, J, H, C, K, D, L
- R_{best} and $m = 2 \Rightarrow$ H, L, D, G, K, C, F, J, B, E, I, A
- R_{best} and $m = 4 \Rightarrow$ H, G, D, L, K, C, F, J, B, E, I, A
- R_{best} and $m = 8 \Rightarrow$ F, E, B, I, J, A, G, C, K, H, D, L

	μ	σ	R_{Sharpe}	R_{best} $(m = 2)$	R_{best} $(m = 4)$	R_{best} $(m = 8)$
A	16%	9%	1.22	2.04	1.88	1.55
B	21%	14%	1.14	2.81	2.42	1.63
C	28%	21%	1.10	3.72	2.82	1.07
D	32%	25%	1.08	4.15	2.90	0.40
E	17%	9%	1.33	2.24	2.08	1.75
F	22%	14%	1.21	3.01	2.62	1.83
G	29%	21%	1.14	3.92	3.04	1.27
H	33%	25%	1.12	4.35	3.10	0.60
I	17%	10%	1.20	2.20	2.00	1.60
J	22%	15%	1.13	2.95	2.50	1.60
K	29%	22%	1.09	3.83	2.86	0.93
L	33%	26%	1.08	4.25	2.90	0.19

$$(26)$$

According to CARA for $m = 4$ the best portfolio is H and according to Sharpe it is E.

9.6   EXTENSION TO NON-GAUSSIAN DISTRIBUTIONS

In the real world the random variables x_i are not Gaussian and one may wonder how this affects our conclusions.

First of all the statement that the Sharpe ratio, the Sortino, the kappa, the omega and the Stutzer index are equivalent is not true any more and each corresponds to a different implicit choice of a utility function. One cannot answer the question to which one is better because there is no objective benchmark any more.

Anyway the real world is "close" to Gaussian if returns are computed over relatively long time periods (this is shown later) and all of these ranking systems are inappropriate in the Gaussian limit. Therefore, there is no reason to believe they should be appropriate for non-Gaussian or close-to-Gaussian distributions.

On the other hand, despite the fact that in the preceding section, equations (20)–(22) and equation (23) are derived assuming a Gaussian $p(x)$, the *ranking induced by equation (23) is still correct for non-Gaussian distributions, providing that one plans to hold portfolio a long enough time.*

First of all it is important to realize that in the Gaussian world equations (20–22) do not depend on the time scale, since the probability distribution for the 1-, the 2- or the 100-day return is always Gaussian. In a non-Gaussian world the probability distribution for 1-day returns is different than the probability distribution for 2-day returns, etc. In order to take this into account we define $p(x)$ as the probability mass function for 1-day returns and, in general, $p_T(X)$ as the probability mass function of

T-day returns where $X = \log(S_T/S_0) = \sum_{i=0}^{i<T} x_i$ and $x_i = \log(S_{i+1}/S_i)$. We will assume all the random variables x_i are independent and follow the distribution p. We also define μ and σ as the mean and standard deviation of p.

We can now rewrite equation (15) as the weighted utility at the end of period T

$$R_W(p, T) = \int_{-\infty}^{+\infty} W(X/T)\,p_T(X)\,dX \qquad (27)$$

Owing to the Central Limit Theorem and the Berry–Esseen Theorem, when $T\to\infty$, p_T approaches a Gaussian distribution with mean μT and standard deviation $\sigma\sqrt{T}$. This is demonstrated in Figure 7 for an initial triangular distribution. Therefore for our choice $W = W_{\text{CARA}}$, equation (27) implies

$$\lim_{T\to\infty} R_{\text{CARA}}(p, T) = -e^{m(r-\mu)+m^2\sigma^2/2} \sim R_{\text{best}}(p) \qquad (28)$$

It remains to address how fast R_{CARA} approaches the limit. From the Berry–Esseen theorem it follows that:

Lemma 1. For every probability mass function p and every $\varepsilon > 0$ there exists a $c > 0$ such that

$$\left| R_{\text{CARA}}(p, T) + e^{m(r-\mu)+m^2\sigma^2/2} \right| < c/\sqrt{T} + \varepsilon \qquad (29)$$

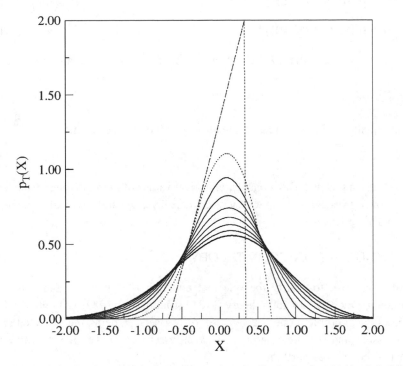

Figure 7 $p_T(x)$ for $T = 1, \ldots, 10$ is shown given a triangular distribution for $p(x)$ (the dashed line). When $T\to\infty$, $p_T(x)$ approaches a Gaussian distribution

where c depends on ε and the shape of p.

Finally from equation (28) and the above lemma we conclude that:

Proposition 2. In the general case of portfolios with random returns having non-Gaussian distributions one should rank the portfolios by explicit integration of equation (27). Nevertheless, for our choice of the CARA utility function and for a long holding period T, this is equivalent to ranking the portfolios using R_{best}, equation (23). The error incurred is proportional to $1/\sqrt{T}$.

9.7   MARKET DETERMINATION OF m

In our notation m is a positive number that encodes the investor's risk tolerance. A low value of m (close to zero) indicates a high tolerance of risk, while a high value of m indicates a low tolerance of risk (risk aversion).

Despite the fact that m is subjective one can ask if there is something like an "average market value" for m. In order to address this question we considered the Dow Jones industrial (*DJI*) average index in the range from Oct 1984 until Oct 2004 and we compute the average yearly return μ and the average yearly volatility σ (standard deviation) of the weekly lognormal returns. We find

$$\mu = 0.1076 (= 10.76\%) \tag{30}$$

$$\sigma = 0.1620 (= 16.20\%) \tag{31}$$

we then assume that the *DJI* has the same ranking as a risk-free interest ($= 0$)

$$R_{best}(DJI) = \frac{\mu}{r} - 1 - m\frac{\sigma^2}{2r} = 0 \tag{32}$$

From equation (32) and a reasonable guess $r \simeq 0.05$ (5%) we obtain

$$m \simeq 4 \tag{33}$$

Therefore, in this paper we consider empirical values of m in the range from 2 (for a risk lover investor) to 8 (for a very risk averse investor) and a typical value $m = 4$ for an average investor.

9.8   MODERN PORTFOLIO THEORY

Finally we wish to clarify the role that equation (23) plays in the context of Markowitz' modern portfolio theory (MPT) (Markowitz, 1952; Wilmott, 2000).

In a typical problem one is given a set of N assets, μ_i being the expected return from asset i and σ_{ij}, the covariance between asset i and j. The risk-free rate is r. What is the optimal portfolio?

The MPT establishes that the optimal portfolio is a combination of the risk-free asset (with weight α) and the Markowitz portfolio (with weight $1 - \alpha$). The

Markowitz portfolio is a linear combination of the assets (excluding the risk-free one) with weights equal to

$$w_i \overset{\text{def}}{=} \sum_j (\sigma^{-1})_{ij}(\mu_j - r) \tag{34}$$

the mean and variance of the Markowitz portfolio are given by

$$\mu_{\text{M}} \overset{\text{def}}{=} \sum_j w_i \mu_i \text{ and } \sigma_{\text{M}} \overset{\text{def}}{=} \sqrt{\sum_j w_i w_j \sigma_{ij}} \tag{35}$$

The MPT decouples the problem of finding the optimal combination of risky assets with that of finding the optimal combination of risk-free asset and risky assets. The MPT solves the first problem but the solution of the second problem is not uniquely determined because it leaves α undetermined.

Since α is not determined by the Markowitz's method, its value is subjective and, in its own way, α measures the attitude towards risk of the investor. We see α is related to our value of m.

Let M_α be a portfolio, which is a linear combination of the risk-free asset with weight α and the Markowitz portfolio (as computed by the MPT) with weight $(1 - \alpha)$. The probability mass function associated to this portfolio is

$$p_\alpha(x) = \alpha\delta(x - r) + (1 - \alpha)\,\frac{1}{\sqrt{2\pi}\sigma_{\text{M}}}e^{-(x-\mu_{\text{M}})^2/2\sigma_{\text{M}}^2} \tag{36}$$

where δ is the Dirac delta function. We can now determine α by maximizing $R_{\text{best}}(p_\alpha)$. This procedure is represented graphically in Figure 8. The solution can be found by explicit computation as stated in the following:

Theorem 1. Given a risk-free rate r and a Markowitz portfolio $(\mu_{\text{M}}, \sigma_{\text{M}})$, according to the R_{best} ranking, the optimal portfolio consists of holding a fraction α of the risk-free asset where

$$\alpha = 1 - \frac{\mu_{\text{M}} - r}{m\sigma_{\text{M}}^2} \tag{37}$$

and a fraction $(1 - \alpha)$ of the Markowitz portfolio. This optimal portfolio has an expected average return and volatility given by

$$\mu_{\text{best}} = r + \frac{(\mu_{\text{M}} - r)^2}{m\sigma_{\text{M}}^2} \text{ and } \sigma_{\text{best}} = \frac{\mu_{\text{M}} - r}{m\sigma_{\text{M}}} \tag{38}$$

Note that the Sharpe ratio cannot be used to solve the problem of determining α for two reasons: (1) the Sharpe ratio is undetermined for the risk-free asset; and (2) in the return versus risk plot the indifference curves associated with constant rankings are straight lines, therefore they cannot be tangent to the Markowitz line parametrized by α.

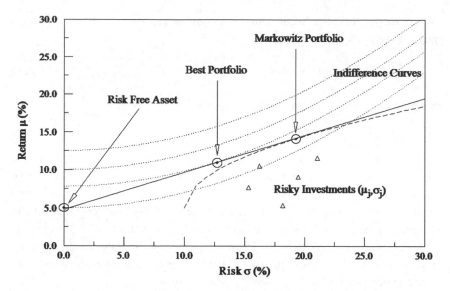

Figure 8   The MPT on a μ, σ plane is shown, where the ranking $R_{best}(p)$ is used to determine the investor's indifference curves. All portfolios on the line are equivalent according to MPT. The concave parabolas represent indifference curves (sets of portfolios having the same ranking). The higher the parabola, the higher the ranking. The best portfolio can be determined by finding the indifference curve tangent to the line or indifference curves. All portfolios on the line are equivalent according to MPT. The concave parabolas represent indifference curves (sets of portfolios having the same ranking). The higher the parabola, the higher the ranking. The best portfolio can be determined by finding the indifference curve tangent to the line figure

9.9 CONCLUSIONS

In this paper we proved that using the Sharpe ratio, the Sortino, the kappa, the omega or the Stutzer index to rank portfolios are equivalent choices when portfolios have Gaussian returns (that eventually is true for sufficiently long time T). Nevertheless, all of these ranking systems implicitly assume a utility function that is not consistent with the risk aversion of investors. Moreover these ranking schemes are not useful for many important practical applications (such as finding indifference curves for use in MPT).

With our choice of the CARA utility function $W(x) = -e^{-m(x-r)}$ (where r is the risk-free rate and m parametrizes our risk attitude) we determined a ranking formula

$$R_{best}(p) = \mu/r - 1 - m\sigma^2/(2r) \tag{39}$$

that is applicable to portfolios with Gaussian and non-Gaussian returns. In the latter case the formula is valid but introduces a numerical error in the ranking that is proportional to $T^{-1/2}$. T is the time one is planning to hold the portfolio. This error can be arbitrarily reduced by holding the portfolio for a sufficiently long time.

Finally, we performed an analysis of the *DJI* average index (data from 1984 until today) and determined an average market value for $m \simeq 4$. Further studies on the time dependence of m and its correlation with other market indicators are required.

According to the EDHEC (Amenc, Malaise, Martellini and Vaisse) 69% of European Hedge Funds reports the Sharpe ratio to their investors and 22% report the Sortino ratio. We believe these numbers are misleading and should be used with caution. In particular:

- One should not at all rank portfolios that are correlated, in this case one should use the MPT or the CAPM models.
- If one is considering a set of uncorrelated portfolios (or portfolios with unknown correlations) in order to select the best and invest funds in both the selected portfolio and the risk-free asset, one should use the Sharpe ratio to rank the portfolios. In this case one also needs to select a utility function to decide how to partition the funds between the selected portfolio and the risk-free asset.
- If one is considering a set of uncorrelated portfolios (or portfolios with unknown correlations) in order to invest a fixed amount of money in the selected portfolio, one should use equation (39).

Some of the ideas discussed in this paper are implemented in the form of computer programs and can be accessed through the web page:

http://www.metacryption.com/schemes.html

REFERENCES

Amenc, N., Malaise, P., Martellini, L. and Vaisse, M., Fund of Hedge Fund Reporting, EDHEC, http://www.edhec.com

Kaplan, P.D. and Knowles, J.A. (2004) Kappa: a generalized downside risk-adjusted performance measure, *Journal of Performance Measurement*, **8**(3).

Kazemi, H., Schneeweis, T. and Gupta, R. (2003) Omega as performance measure, *CISDM 2003, Proceedings*.

Markowitz, H.M. (1952) Portfolio selection, *Journal of Finance*, **7**(1), 77–91.

Shadwick, W. and Keating, C. (2002) A universal performance measure, *Journal of Performance Measurement*, (Spring) **6**(3).

Sharpe, W.F. (1964) Capital asset prices: a theory of market equilibrium under conditions of risk, *Journal of Finance*, **19**(3), 425–442.

Sortino, F.A. (2001) From alpha to omega, *Managing Downside Risk in Financial Markets*, F.A. Sortino and S.E. Satchell (eds), Reed Educational and Professional Publishing Ltd.

Sortino, F.A. and Forsey, H.J. (1996) On the use and misuse of downside risk, *Journal of Portfolio Management*, **22**(2), 35–42.

Sortino, F.A. and Price, L.N. (1994) Performance measurement in a downside risk framework, *Journal of Investing*, **3**(3), 59–64.

Sortino, F.A. and Van Der Meer, R. (1991) Downside risk, *Journal of Portfolio Management*, **17**(4), 27–32.

Stutzer, M. (2000) A portfolio performance index, *Financial Analysts Journal*, **56** May/June.

Wilmott, P. (2000) *On Quantitative Finance*, Wiley, New York.

Index

(n = footnote)

Accountant, 80, 82, 83
Accounting, 82–4
Active commodity strategies
  commodity futures investments, 32–3
Annual return, 56
Arbitrage-free pricing principles, 16
Asian demand and energy infrastructure
  petroleum complex, 34–5
Asset-Backed Securities (ABS), 13
Asset swaps, 3–4

Back office careers
  accounting, 82–4
  customer service, 84–5
  human resources, 85–7
  legal, 87–8
  systems/information technology, 88–9
Backwardation, 30n
Barreau, J.-M., xi, 64
Base metals
  super cycle in copper, 35–6, 37
Berry–Esseen theorem, 129, 139
Bond plus call option, 66, 68
Butterfly, 5

Capital structure arbitrage, 8–9
Careers, hedge funds, 90
  back office careers, 82–9
  front office careers, 93–8
  middle office careers, 90–3
  strategies and profiles, 100–1
  women, special issues, 98–9
Cash-out refinance, 11n, 20

Cayman Islands, setting up
  registration
    with CIMA, 56–9
    with registrar of companies, 54–6
  signing offshore
    while being onshore, 59–60
  SPC, 60–2
  tax exemption
    timeline and application, 59
Cayman Islands Monetary Authority
  (CIMA), 47–8, 49, 54n, 55, 56–59, 61
Cayman mutual funds, 47
Chief executive officer (CEO), 81, 95
Chief financial officer (CFO), 80, 82,
  83, 90
Chief information officer (CIO), 80, 88
Chief operations officer (COO), 81, 90
Chief technology officer (CTO), 88
Client relations, 84–5
Collateralized Mortgage Obligation
  (CMO), 11, 13, 15, 16, 18, 23
Commercial loans, 13
Commercial Mortgage Backed Securities
  (CMBS), 13, 14
Commodity futures investments
  absolute returns, 25
  global supply shocks and inflation,
    34–6
    base metals, 35–6
    monetary stimulus, excessive, 36, 38
    petroleum complex, 34–5
  investing interest
    return compression, 26–8

risk management
   downside risk protection, 36–9
   payoff profiles and sizing, 39–40
   structural returns
      due to hedging pressure, 29–33
      due to supply usage imbalances, 28–9
Compliance, 80, 83, 84, 87, 93
Conforming loans, 14
Constant proportion portfolio insurance
   (CPPI), 66, 68, 69, 70, 71, 73
Contango, 30n
Contractual priorities, 9
Convertible arbitrage, 115, 117, 124
Copper, super cycle, 35–6, 37
Corporate bond arbitrage, 5–8
   bond basis trading, 7
Correlation trading, *see* Index correlation
   trading
Coupon payment, 4
Cowboys, 96
Credit risk, 6, 12, 13, 21, 23, 24
Curtailment, 12n
Customer service, 80, 84–5

Default and recovery models, 21
Delta one products, *see* Tracker products
Developers, IT, 80, 88
Distressed securities, 115, 117, 123
Dow Jones AIG Commodity Index
   (DJ-AIGCI), 29
Dow Jones industrial (DJI) average index,
   140, 142
Dubrovay, J., xi, 64
Due diligence, 46, 49–50
Dynamic leveraging, 68, 74
Dynamic structures, *see* Constant
   proportion portfolio insurance

Emerging markets, 95, 100, 115, 123
Energy infrastructure and Asian demand
   petroleum products, 34–5
Equity market neutral, 95, 100, 114, 115,
   123, 124
Equivalence, 129

Fixed capital formation, 35–6
Fixed income arbitrage
   asset swaps, 3–4
   capital structure arbitrage, 8–10

corporate bond arbitrage, 5–8
government issued debt, 1–3
yield curve arbitrage, 4–5
FNMA 5-year security, 4
Form MF1, 49, 57
Forward yield curve, 5
Front office careers
   marketing, 93–4
   quantitative modelers, 94
   traders, 95–8
Fund of funds hedge fund, 96
Fund regulation, 46–51

Gaussian world, equivalence, 130–3
General counsel, 80, 87
Global macro, 95, 100, 115, 116, 117, 118,
   120, 121, 122
Goldman Sachs Commodity Index
   (GSCI), 29, 32
Government issued debt
   basis trading, 1–2
   issue trading, 2–3
Graham, K.A., xii, 80, 96n, 101n
Gunzberg, J., xii, 25

Hedge fund
   careers
      back office, 80, 82–9
      front office, 81, 89, 93–8
      middle office, 80–1, 90–3
      strategies and profiles, 100–1
      women, special issues, 98–101
   going offshore
      Cayman Islands, setting up,
         43, 54
      considerations, 43
   investing, caution, 112
   leverage, 1, 22, 23, 65, 66, 68, 71–2
   liquidity haircut, 102, 110, 111
   return compression, 26–8
   strategy, 1, 17, 45, 74, 91, 96, 97, 106,
      114, 116, 118, 122
   structured products, 64, 65
Hedge Fund Asset, 64, 66, 67, 68, 69, 70,
   73, 74, 75, 76, 77, 81
Hedge fund investing, caution
   available data, 112, 113–14, 126
   combination with equity, 123–4
   diversification, 126

investment, 40, 67, 112
modern portfolio theory, 124
mortgage backed security, 12n
risks, 102, 117–18
Sharpe ratios and alphas, 119–20
shortcuts, 120–2
similar indices and various index
  providers, 116–17
strategy and behaviour difference
  classification, 114–16
Hedging pressure, structural returns
active commodity strategies, 32–3
futures markets
  Hicks hypothesis, 30–1
  Keynes hypothesis, 29–30
returns
  spot commodity prices, 31–2
Hedging strategies
and risk management, 23–4
Hicks, J.R., 30, 31n
High water mark, 103, 104, 105,
  106, 108
Human resources, 80, 85, 86, 87

Illiquidity premium, simulation, 107
Index arbitrage, 7
Index correlation trading, 7
Industrial revolution
in China, 35–6
Interest-rate neutral, 23
Inverse floaters, 16, 23
Inverse interest-only bonds, 16
Investing, words of caution, 112
Investment level, 69, 70, 71
Investor
allocation decrease, 106–7
profit and loss function, 107
protection, 47, 51
relations, 80, 84, 85
Investor's risk tolerance
market determination, 140

Jumbo mortgages, 14, 15

Kappa-*n* ratio, 130
Kat, H.M., xii, 112, 114, 117
Keynes, J.M., 29–30
Keynesian effects, 33
Krishnan, H.P., xiii, 102

Laws, 44–5
Lead developer, 88
Legal, 87–8
Leveraged structures, 68
Liquidity and leverage, 21–2
Liquidity haircut
illiquidity premium, simulation, 107–11
Longstaff's method, 106–7
valuing manager's contract, 103–5
Liquidity risk, 103, 119–20
Long/short equity, 96, 100, 114, 124
Longstaff's method, 103, 106–7

Managed Accounts, 64, 73, 75, 76, 78
Manager's contract
valuing, 103–5
Market-neutral strategies, 18
Marketing, 93–4
and listing considerations, 52–3
Marking-to-market problems, 22–3, 117,
  119–20
Markowitz portfolio, 141
Maturity-priority debt, 9
Mean–variance optimizations, 102, 110,
  124, 125
Mems & arts, 43, 53, 55–6, 60
Merger arbitrage, 95, 115, 123
Middle office careers
operations, 90
research, 91–2
risk management, 92–3
Modern portfolio theory (MPT), 124–5,
  129, 140–2
Monetary stimulus, excessive, 38
global supply shock and inflation, 36
Mortgage hedge fund investing
analytic methods and models, 18–21
  default and recovery models, 21
  option-adjusted spread analysis, 19–20
  prepayment models, 20–1
  static analysis, 19
diversity, 11
hedging strategies and risk management
  credit, 23–4
  interest rates, 23
  model error, 24
  spread, 23
  volatility, 23
liquidity and leverage, 21–2

mortgage loans, varieties, 13–15
mortgage-backed securities, varieties,
    15–16
mortgage mechanics, basic, 12–13
net asset value
    and marking to market, 22–3
strategies' varieties, 16–18
    hedge fund strategies' categories,
        17–18
Mosevich, J.W., xiii, 128
Multi-strategy hedge fund, 96

Nelken, I., xiii, 102
New industrial revolution
    in China
        base metals, 35–6
Non-conforming mortgages, 14, 15
Non-Gaussian distributions, extension,
    138–40
Normal backwardation hypothesis, 29–30,
    31n

Oil, super spike, 34–5
Omega ratio, 130
On ranking schemes and portfolio
        selection, 128
    Gaussian world, equivalence, 130–4
    investor's risk tolerance
        market determination, 140
    modern portfolio theory, 140–2
    non-Gaussian distributions, extension,
        138–40
    ranking and risk aversion, 134–5
    utility function, 136–8
Operations manager, 90
Operations specialists, 90
Optimal portfolio, 140–1
Option-adjusted spread (OAS) analysis,
    19–20
Overseas marketing, 53–4
Oversight, reputation, 46–51

Paradise for speculators, 25
Pass-through products, *see* Tracker
    products
PCC, *see* Protected cell company
Petroleum complex
    super spike in oil, 34–5

Di Pierro, M., xiii–xiv, 128
Prepayment models, 20–1
Principal protection structures
    bond plus call option, 68
    constant proportion portfolio insurance,
        69–70
Privacy protection, 53
Programmers, 88
Project managers, 89
Proprietary trading firm, 96
Protected cell company (PCC), 61n

Quantitative modelers, 94

Rachlin, E., xiv, 1
Ranking, 129
    and risk aversion, 134–5
Recruiters, 86
Reference level (RL), 69
    fixed at inception, 70–2
Registered mutual fund, 48, 57
Reputation, 44–5, 46–51, 91
Residential loans, 13
Return compression, 26–8

Segregated Portfolio Company (SPC), 46,
    60–2
Sharpe ratio, 102, 119–20, 126, 129–30,
    134–5, 136, 141, 143
Sherak, R., xiv, 11
Single strategy hedge fund, 96
Sortino ratio, 130
SPC, *see* Segregated Portfolio Company
Spot commodity prices
    commodity futures investment, 25, 31–2
Static analysis, 19
Static structures, *see* Bond plus call option
Strip, 16
Structural returns
    hedging pressure
        active commodity strategies, 32–3
        Hicks hypothesis, 30–1
        Keynes hypothesis, 29–30
        spot commodity prices, 31–2
        supply usage imbalances, 28–9
Structured products (SPs)
    basics, 64
    evolution, 64–6

key value drivers
  liquidity, 75
  product structure, 76–7
  risk management, 75–6
  tax treatment, 77
  underlying fund, 74
looking ahead, 77–9
types
  leveraged structure, 68
  principal protection structures,
    68–72
  tracker products, 66–7
usage, 72–3
Stutzer index, 130
Supply usage imbalances
  structural returns, 28–9
System architect, 88
Systems/information technology, 88–9

Tax exemption, application, 59
Taxes, 44–5
Till, H., xiv–xv, 25
Timeline, 59
To Be Announced (TBA), 15n
  market, 15
Tracker products, 66–7
Traders, 95–8
Transfer agent, 50

US mortgage market, 11

Woerheide, C., xv–xvi, 43
Women, special issues, 98–9

Yield curve arbitrage, 4–5

Zero coupon bond (ZCB), 64–5, 68, 69